Colorado's
CONTINENTAL
DIVIDE

Colorado's
CONTINENTAL
DIVIDE
A HIKING AND BACKPACKING GUIDE

Ron Ruhoff

CORDILLERA PRESS, INC.

Publishers in the Rockies

Library of Congress Cataloging-in-Publication Data
Ruhoff, Ron, 1938-
    Colorado's continental divide : a hiking and backpacking guide / Ron Ruhoff.
      p.   cm.
    Bibliography: p.
    Includes index.
    ISBN 0-917895-26-6 : $9.95
    1. Hiking — Colorado — Guide-books.
    2. Hiking — Continental Divide Trail — Guide-books.
    3. Backpacking — Colorado — Guide-books.
    4. Backpacking — Continental Divide Trail — Guide-books.
    5. Colorado — Description and travel — 1981- — Guide-books.
    6. Continental Divide Trail — Guide-books.
    I. Title.
GV199.42.C6R85   1988
917.88 — dc19   89-640
                                          CIP

First Printing
    1 2 3 4 5 6 7 8 9

Printed in the United States of America.

Front Cover Photograph
North of Rollins Pass. Ron Ruhoff
Back Cover Photograph
Atop Hagar Mountain. Fred Giesel
Cover Design
Richard M. Kohen
Design & Typography
Richard M. Kohen, Shadow Canyon Graphics — Evergreen, Colorado

Cordillera Press, Inc.
Post Office Box 3699
Evergreen, Colorado 80439
(303) 670-3010

Table of Contents

For Bruce, Dori, Eric, Fred, Hugh, Jay,

Jerry, Jim, Joe, Mark, Pam, Roger, Sid, and Steve.

and in memory of

Dr. Gerald Coon, Cedric Damewood,

and Helen Giesel.

Climbing Colorado's Great Divide

The spirit of the high mountains becomes a part of you up here —
The top of this great backbone of our land –
the Continental Divide.
It's a place of lonely beauty,
The home of rocky summits, alpine flowers and
prevailing west winds of the freshest air.
This is a place to feel kin to the soaring birds
and the clouds themselves.
A place to share magnificent views with climbing companions.
The divide is a place which grows on you
and beckons you to return —
again and again.

— Ron Ruhoff

About the Author

Ron Ruhoff is a veteran photographer and outdoorsman who has spent more than thirty years hiking and photographing the many wonders of Colorado. His "photomusical adventures," slide programs combining music and spectacular scenery, have delighted tens of thousands since he began them in 1960. One can hardly pick up a Colorado calendar or stack of postcards without finding at least one of his many photographs. Ruhoff has long shared his many interests with classes on Colorado history and photography at Red Rocks and Front Range community colleges. Ruhoff lives in Evergreen with his wife, Pam, and children, Chrystal, James, and Anna, all enthusiastic backpackers and hikers. ▲

Acknowledgements

Most of the information needed for hikes along the continental divide was obtained from U. S. Geological Survey maps and U. S. Forest Service maps. I want to thank the Evergreen Regional Library of Jefferson County for the use of their fine collection of Colorado maps while compiling the mileage lists. Thanks also go to Mary Larsgaard of the Arthur Lakes Library of the Colorado School of Mines for help with maps of other parts of the continent. Their world collection of survey maps made it possible to plot the course of the divide throughout Alaska, Canada, the United States, Mexico, and Central America.

Because I have not hiked the entire divide in Colorado myself, invaluable information was obtained from a number of people who have hiked the entire distance. I gratefully thank the following hikers for allowing me to visit with them as well as make use of their photographs: Douglas Barr, Jim Beblavi, Mark Bonomo, Gary McKay, Tom and Judy Melzer, Dr. Robert Melzer, David Miller, Wes and Mary Mauz, and Doug and Ellen Stewart. All were a great pleasure to meet and the time spent discussing our common interest was most enjoyable and rewarding.

One of the most perplexing problems encountered in plotting the course of the divide through North America concerned the question of whether or not the high volcanoes of Mexico, Popocatepetl and Ixtacihuatl, are actually on the divide ridge. The divide is simply not plotted on most maps of Mexico. Credit must be given to the H. M. Gousha Company for publishing a Conoco road map — the only map I could find that shows in detail the divide coinciding with those two mountains. In addition, I wish to thank longtime mountain climber Miguel A. Najera of Mexico City for his research on the problem and the contribution of his photography to illustrate those highest points on the divide in North America.

Numerous books were also helpful in obtaining historical information and they are included in the recommended reading list in the bibliography. ▲

Introduction

A Summons to the Divide

Early in 1963, President John F. Kennedy urged the people of the United States to "get in shape" and test their fitness with a fifty-mile hike. As an avid mountain climber and hiker, I found the idea intriguing and began discussing it with my friend and co-worker, Hugh Mayes. We agreed to make such a hike together, but also decided to make our outing something unusual. Since we both preferred the mountain country, our first thought was to travel the highest fifty miles we could find — the kind of terrain Colorado could easily supply.

During the spring of 1963, Hugh and I looked over maps and trails and decided that the continental divide would be a logical place for a high fifty miles. For a starter, Hugh and I picked the section between Fremont and Loveland passes in central Colorado, a distance of fifty winding miles. The average elevation was about as high as could be found and the route even included the only 14,000-foot peaks squarely on the continental divide — Grays and Torreys peaks.

While searching for a specific segment to hike, another goal occurred to us. Why not attempt to walk the entire length of the continental divide in Colorado, right on the ridge itself, with one foot on the Pacific side and one on the Atlantic! Now, as I compile this story from my journals, I realize that others have in fact done just that and hiked the entire continental divide from one end of Colorado to the other. But in 1963, the challenge to do so was a clarion summons.

Although a trail system on the order of the well-known Appalachian Trail has yet to be completed along the continental divide, there is a general trail system which parallels much of the divide. The Colorado Mountain Club, the Continental Divide Trail Society, and other organizations have done much over the years to promote the construction and marking of connecting trails so that a continuous trail route is generally available along the Colorado divide. Additionally, in 1988, the "Colorado Trail" was completed linking

Denver to Durango and it also parallels certain portions of the divide.

Our goal, however, was more unusual than following trails and required us to stay on the actual divide ridge as much as possible. Because this involves some difficult ridge hopping, it is a very different kind of experience from trail hiking. Only a handful of people have hiked the entire distance of Colorado's continental divide in this manner. The pioneers in this sort of expedition were Carl and Robert Melzer and Julius Johnson, who made the first complete hike of Colorado's divide in 1936.

As it turned out, my personal divide hiking experience comes to roughly one hundred miles, pieced together from many outings over almost twenty years. For those who are fortunate enough to have jobs or school situations allowing an entire summer free, the possibilities for hiking a large portion, or even the entire length of the divide, are numerous. I always had to be content with weekends and an occasional four-day trip. Whatever method you choose, the most important thing is your personal goal, whatever it might be, and the enjoyment you get from the experience and the companionship along the way. Those are the things that really count in any outdoor adventure.

Special concerns about this kind of divide hiking are addressed throughout the book, but three are important enough to emphasize here. First, like any type of off-trail activity, divide hiking has an impact on the fragile alpine environment. Low-impact camping and hiking are absolute requirements for anyone traveling Colorado's divide. Packing out all trash, avoiding campfires, and properly disposing of personal wastes are mandatory and will help keep Colorado's divide country pristine.

Second, Colorado's high country is notorious for rapid weather changes and frequent adverse conditions. A typical mountain climb finds one leaving base camp early in the morning, reaching the summit before the afternoon storms set in, and then returning to the starting point. On the divide, however, you are on high ridges constantly, at times carrying overnight gear, and you must always be prepared to "get off," sometimes into unfamiliar country because of lightning and storm dangers.

Finally, as with all outdoor activities, the users of this guide are reminded that they assume the risk for their activities and that common sense and a recognition of their individual limits and abilities is essential.

Whether you embark on an expedition to hike all of Colorado's great continental divide or whether you simply enjoy an hour's stroll atop one of Colorado's high passes, I hope that the following stories and accompanying descriptions and charts will be entertaining and informative. Perhaps we'll meet some day up on that high, lonesome ridge. When I began my divide quest back in 1963, I became somewhat obsessed with it. I know that I'll be back for more! ▲

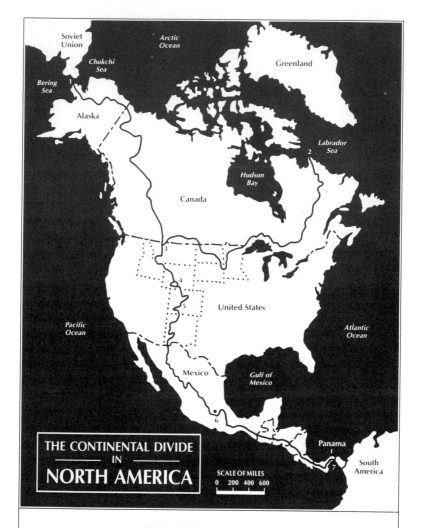

POINTS OF INTEREST

1. Bering Strait at Wales, Alaska. *Beginning of Pacific-Atlantic/Arctic divide.*
2. Cape Chidley, New Foundland. *Beginning of Atlantic-Arctic Divide.*
3. Triple Divide Peak, Montana. *Only point of division for three oceans.*
4. Great Divide Basin.
5. Grays Peak, Colorado. *Highest point on divide in USA and Canada.*
6. Mexico City and the high volcanoes.
7. Panama. *End of the Continental Divide in North America.*

(**Note:** *Contiguous states that touch the divide are shown by dotted lines.*)

Part I
The Divide on a Continental Scale

Although this guide deals primarily with Colorado's portion of the continental divide, a description of the major features of the entire divide in North America is important to that story. All continents are surrounded by oceans. The division lines for the rivers draining each continent are usually known and mapped. The term "continental divide," as used in the United States, is generally associated with the Rocky Mountains, which divide the drainages to either the Pacific or Atlantic watersheds. But there is much more to it than that.

My friend, Tom Cox, who has a summer home in Detroit Lakes, Minnesota, loves to tell people that he lives on the "continental divide." Most think he is joking, but he is quite right. The North American continent is surrounded by three oceans — Arctic, Atlantic, and Pacific, and there are dividing lines which separate the three watersheds. The tri-division point is a mountain named Triple Divide Peak, located in the center of Glacier National Park, Montana.

The well-known continental divide heads south from this peak through the Rocky Mountain states, Mexico, and Central America to Panama. This divide also goes north from Triple Divide Peak through the Canadian Rockies, the Yukon Territory, and Alaska to the Bering Sea. The lesser known divide separates the Hudson Bay/Arctic Ocean drainage from that of the Atlantic and heads east from Triple Divide Peak. The Hudson Bay divide wanders through the relatively flat country of Montana, Alberta, Saskatchewan, North Dakota, South Dakota, Minnesota, Ontario, and Quebec. Cape Chidley, Newfoundland, is the point where the Arctic meets the Atlantic.

South America's continental divide is really an extension of the same rift in the earth's crust that follows the great Andes Mountain Range all the way from Panama to Cape Horn. Together, the continental divide in North and South America makes the greatest divide in the world, a length of some 13,000 miles from Wales,

Alaska, to Cape Horn. What a divide hike that would make!

From Wales, Alaska, where on a clear day one can see the Soviet Union across the Bering Strait, the continental divide heads east through the Seward Peninsula. This is where a land bridge once connected Asia with North America. The Bering Strait is the northernmost portion of the Pacific Ocean. North of the Bering Strait the Arctic Ocean begins with the Chukchi Sea. Some maps have shown the divide beginning farther north at Point Hope, but most agree on the Bering Strait as the starting point.

The Alaskan portion of the divide first crosses the York Mountains and then swings far to the north, passing through the Brooks Range. The northernmost latitude of the divide is nearly 70° N. in the Romanzof Mountains, where the Arctic National Wildlife Refuge is located. Nowhere in Alaska does the elevation of the divide reach much over 8,000 feet, as the great peaks of Mount McKinley and the St. Elias Range are far to the south of the divide.

The divide enters Canada in the northern portion of the Yukon Territory, where it becomes associated with the Rocky Mountains throughout the rest of Canada and the United States. The divide continues south through British Columbia and becomes the boundary line between this province and Alberta all the way to the Montana border. Along the way, Jasper, Banff, Yoho, and Kootenay national parks offer the highest and most spectacular portions of the divide ridge in Canada. Glacial activity is intense in this area, making for some of the most rugged mountain scenery in all of North America. Mount Robson, at 12,972 feet, is the highest peak in the Canadian Rockies, but is located some distance west of the actual divide ridge.

The divide enters the contiguous United States through the Waterton Lakes-Glacier International Peace Park. This is the only joint park system in the world. Waterton Lakes National Park in Alberta was established in 1895 and Glacier National Park in Montana was set aside in 1910. In 1932, the unique international status was achieved through the efforts of the Rotary International organizations of Montana and Alberta.

Glacier National Park offers some of the most spectacular mountain scenery in the United States. A single transpark road, called Going-to-the-Sun Highway, allows visitors to drive across the divide at 6,664-foot Logan Pass. Along the route many jagged

Divide Mountain, 8,647 feet, stands alone on the left, reflected in St. Marys Lake, Glacier National Park. It is the last true mountain on the Hudson Bay Divide before the divide heads east across the plains. Divide Mountain is a survey point squarely on the eastern park boundary. Ron Ruhoff

peaks are visible as well as the beautiful Garden Wall, which forms a portion of the divide ridge.

Midway through the park, Triple Divide Peak's 8,011 foot summit marks the only place in North America where three ocean watersheds are separated. Here the waters flow either to the Atlantic, Pacific, or Hudson Bay/Arctic drainages. From Triple Divide Peak, the division line between Arctic and Atlantic wanders east through relatively flat country and is rarely shown on maps. I found it necessary to plot most of this divide by tracing through the headwaters of rivers as they drain toward one watershed or the other.

After leaving Glacier Park, the Arctic/Atlantic divide runs northeast past Lethbridge, Alberta, where the Milk River drains south to the Missouri and the South Saskatchewan River carries water toward Hudson Bay. Crossing southern Saskatchewan, the divide suddenly dips south into northwestern North Dakota, passing just south of Minot. For some distance, the divide separates the Sheyenne and James rivers. The James meets the Missouri at Yankton, South Dakota, while the Sheyenne joins the Red River of the North near

Split Mountain, 8,781 feet, dominates the center of this view from Red Eagle Lake in Glacier National Park. The high peak in the distance to the left is Norris Mountain, 8,876 feet. Triple Divide Peak, 8,011 feet, is the slight hump on the left (east) ridge of Norris and is the only spot in North America where water is divided between three oceans. Linda Neuberg

Fargo, North Dakota. The divide crosses a portion of South Dakota just before entering Minnesota at the large bump in that state's western border formed by Lake Traverse and Big Stone Lake.

Lake Traverse is the source of the Bois de Sioux River, which eventually becomes the Red River of the North. Big Stone Lake is the source of the Minnesota River which joins the Mississippi River near Minneapolis. The little town of Browns Valley, Minnesota, virtually lies on the divide at the western border of Minnesota.

On its way through Minnesota, the Arctic/Atlantic divide passes just east of Fergus Falls, near Detroit Lakes, then about five miles west of Lake Itasca, source of the Mississippi River. When the divide reaches Hibbing, Minnesota, near the Mesabi Iron Range, another divide branches off toward the southeast — the divide of waters going to either the Mississippi River or Lake Superior and the St. Lawrence River drainage.

The main Arctic/Atlantic divide continues through the northeast arm of Minnesota and enters Canada once again in the province of Ontario. Nipigon, Ontario, and Labrador City, Newfoundland,

Mount Gould, 9,541 feet, rises in the background in this view from the Continental Divide Trail along the Garden Wall in Glacier National Park.
Linda Neuberg

The continental divide runs atop the beautiful Garden Wall as it rises above the Going-to-the-Sun Highway in Glacier National Park. Linda Neuberg

are on the divide as it becomes the boundary between Quebec and Newfoundland. Finally, the end point is reached at Cape Chidley, Newfoundland.

Back on Triple Divide Peak, the main continental divide heads south. Marias Pass is a key crossing of the divide just south of Glacier National Park. U.S. 2 shares this 5,215-foot pass with the Burlington Northern Railroad. Marias Pass is the lowest crossing of the divide in the contiguous United States. Soon the divide becomes the Idaho-Montana border through the extremely rough Bitteroot Range, where it crosses several peaks above 10,000 feet. As the divide enters Yellowstone National Park, three states share a common point — Wyoming, Idaho, and Montana. Granite Peak, 12,799 feet, is Montana's highest summit, but it is located far east of the divide near Red Lodge.

Entering Wyoming, the divide passes about five miles south of Old Faithful Geyser and then circles the southern end of Yellowstone Lake as it traverses the country's oldest national park. The divide then follows the rugged Wind River Range, where many peaks tower over 13,000 feet in elevation. Wyoming has fifty-one peaks over 13,000 feet. Gannett Peak's 13,804-foot summit tops them all and lies directly on the continental divide in the center of the Bridger Wilderness. The Grand Teton, although far west of the divide, is Wyoming's second highest peak at 13,767 feet. Most of the other thirteeners are found on and around the divide as it passes through the Wind River Range, including Downs Peak, 13,344; Pedestal Peak, 13,340; Flagstone Peak, 13,450; Bastion Peak, 13,494; Rampart Peak, 13,500; Mount Koven, 13,265; Gannett Peak, 13,804; Mount Woodrow Wilson, 13,502; The Sphinx, 13,258; Dinwoody Peak, 13,400; and Mount Helen, 13,620.

The divide then drops south to South Pass, the venerable 7,550-foot crossing of the Rockies used by the Oregon Trail. Nearby, South Pass City and Atlantic City were once bustling mining towns. One of the most unusual features of the continental divide begins just a few miles south of South Pass. Here, the divide splits and surrounds the Great Divide Basin, also known as the Red Desert. This oval basin measures some fifty by seventy miles in size and is a true desert with no natural outlet. Within the basin are several sand dune areas, known as the Ferris and Kilpecker dunes. The separate ridges of the divide come together again at Bridger Pass,

Gannett Peak dominates the view northwest from Turret Peak and is perhaps the most alpine peak in the contiguous United States. Water from its many glaciers flows into the Green River on the west and the Wind River on the east. Carl Blaurock

about fifteen miles south of Rawlins.

The divide runs along the Sierra Madre Range in southern Wyoming and northern Colorado. The last high point before entering Colorado is the 11,007-foot summit of Bridger Peak, named for the well-known explorer, mountain man, and guide. The Sierra Madre, Park, and Rabbit Ears ranges offer relatively easy country prior to the divide's entrance into Rocky Mountain National Park, Colorado's largest. Popular Trail Ridge Road crosses the divide at 10,758-foot Milner Pass between Estes Park and Grand Lake. The highest point on the divide in Rocky Mountain National Park is 13,327-foot McHenrys Peak. Longs Peak, 14,255 feet, is Colorado's northernmost fourteener and most popular climb, but it is situated two miles east of the divide ridge.

Immediately south of Rocky Mountain National Park is the rugged Arapaho Range, also called the Indian Peaks. Most of the major summits lie directly on the divide and make a formidable section for those considering a hike along the divide ridge. Many of those who have hiked the divide agree that this area should be

From I-70 at Genesee Park, the continental divide dominates the view west, from left to right, Colorado Mines Peak, Mount Flora, Witter Peak, Mount Eva, Parry Peak, Mount Bancroft, and James Peak. Chrystal Ruhoff

skirted. The Arapaho Peaks, Navajo, Apache, Arikaree, Shoshoni, Toll, and Paiute peaks are best climbed individually.

Between Rollins and Berthoud passes, the divide, including prominent 13,294-foot James Peak, provides one of the most often viewed and photographed scenes in Colorado. Travelers driving west from Denver on I-70 stop at Genesee Park to view the Denver Mountain Park's buffalo herd and this portion of the divide which looms in the distance. The single-span bridge that crosses I-70 at this location was designed to frame the view of the continental divide as one drives under it.

Colorado has its own unique spot on the continental divide in the form of Grays Peak, just west of Georgetown. At 14,270 feet, Grays Peak is the highest point on the divide in the United States and Canada. Nearby Torreys Peak, 14,267 feet, is the only other 14,000-foot summit actually on the divide ridge in Colorado, even though there are fifty-four fourteeners in the state. Throughout Colorado, the divide winds and twists a total of 673 miles through the Front, Mosquito, Sawatch, Cochetopa Hills, La Garita, and San Juan mountain ranges.

Ixtacihuatl, "the white woman," lies in repose above El Sacromonte in Amecameca, Mexico. Miguel A. Najera

Popocatepetl, 17,887 feet, is the highest point on the continental divide in North America. This view is from 12,950 feet at the lodge at Tlamacas. Miguel A. Najera

The continental divide enters New Mexico just west of Chama and follows generally low country through the western portions of the state. The most mountainous section of the divide is the Black Range, where Allegros Peak offers the highest point at 10,244 feet. Other peaks in the 9,000-foot class are found in the Gila National Forest where the Mangas, Long Canyon, and Elk ranges form the divide. Wheeler Peak, 13,160 feet, is the highest summit in New Mexico, but it is located near Taos and well east of the divide.

The divide ridge leaves the United States through the southwestern corner of New Mexico and enters Chihuahua, Mexico. Locating its exact route through Mexico is difficult, as most maps of the country do not show it at all. Even the national topographic maps of Mexico do not indicate the continental divide! The only detailed map I have found that indicates the divide clearly through Mexico is one published by the H. M. Gousha Company as a Conoco road map.

The highest mountains of Mexico rise in the vicinity of Mexico City in the form of volcanic peaks. The continental divide crosses Popocatepetl, 17,887 feet, and Ixtacihuatl, 17,343 feet, making these mountains the highest points on the divide in all of North America. A number of other 14,000 and 15,000-foot mountains are also found in the area. Ixtacihuatl is a very beautiful mountain, and when covered with snow, it resembles a woman's figure lying down, hence the Aztec name meaning "white woman." Popocatepetl means "smoking mountain" and last erupted with ash in 1943.

The highest peak in Mexico is Citlaltepetl, often called Orizaba, 18,701 feet. Citlaltepetl is not on the divide, however, but is located thirty miles northwest of the city of Orizaba. This high volcano is the third highest mountain in North America, topped only by Mount McKinley in Alaska and Mount Logan in the Yukon Territory.

As the divide continues south, there are no mountains as high as 14,000 feet either in Mexico or Central America. The highest peak in Central America is the Tajumulco volcano in Guatamala which reaches 13,845 feet. At the Isthmus of Panama, the land joining the continents of North and South America is only fifty miles wide. Here, the Panama Canal was constructed by the United States and when completed in 1914, it allowed ocean going ships to cross over the continental divide from one ocean to the other. Ships could save 7,800 miles on journeys that once had to go completely around South America at Cape Horn. The actual crossing of the divide takes place at the Gaillard Cut, a channel leading out of Gatun Lake, at an elevation of eighty-five feet above sea level.

The California gold rush of 1849 prompted the construction of the Panama Railroad, which was completed across the isthmus in 1855, allowing the transfer of passengers and freight in a more efficient manner between the east and west coasts of the United States. The railroad served that purpose well until the United States completed its own transcontinental railroad in 1869. The Union Pacific Railroad crosses a relatively low portion of the divide just west of Rawlins, Wyoming, along the southern portion of the Great Divide Basin.

South America's Andes Range is a whole story in itself with numerous mountains 18,000 to 22,000 feet high. Aconcagua, at 22,835 feet, is the highest of them all and is located in Argentina. Aconcagua has the distinction of being the highest mountain in both the western and southern hemispheres. Finally, Cape Horn is reached, the southern terminus of the great divide. Antarctica is only 600 miles away and the Atlantic and Pacific oceans mingle here. ▲

Webster Pass and 12,801-foot Red Cone rise above the iron springs of Handcart Gulch. Ron Ruhoff

Part II

One Man's Divide:
A Personal Adventure

Fremont Pass to Georgia Pass, July 1963

There used to be a tiny restaurant near the telephone building in downtown Denver that served the most delicious chili one could imagine. Hugh Mayes and I spent many a lunch hour there early in 1963, discussing plans for our upcoming fifty-mile hike. Having selected the section of the continental divide between Fremont and Loveland passes as our goal, it was time to get down to the nittygritty details of what gear we would need, how much time would be required, and who would help with the driving. Our work schedules allowed us an occasional four-day weekend, so we assumed this would be adequate — a twelve or thirteen mile per day average didn't sound at all unreasonable.

I contacted my close friend Cedric Damewood, better known to his friends as "Uncle Dudley," to help us with our plans. Ced had recently retired from his job as a printer with the *Rocky Mountain News*, but I had known him since we met in the Mile-Hi Jeep Club in 1957. He loved to drive his little red jeep all over the Colorado mountains and usually found his favorite country right around the very section of the divide that we planned to hike.

Ced was delighted with our plans and invited Hugh and me to his home to go over maps and itinerary. As we poured over U.S. Geological Survey maps covering the area of our hike, we soon realized that Uncle Dudley knew just about every inch of that area by heart. He quickly volunteered to drive for us, carrying our camp gear and food as necessary. We planned to hike from Fremont Pass to Hoosier Pass on the first day, and from Hoosier to Boreas Pass or beyond on the second; the remaining time and distance would go according to how we felt.

We scheduled four days off in mid-July 1963 and began gathering our equipment and supplies. Although I had been mountain climbing and camping for many years, I had not done any overnight backpacking and had to find a suitable pack to use for the longer sections of the hike. For this occasion, I borrowed an early model Kelty from my longtime climbing friend, Mike Sadusky. I already had a day pack, Primus stove, air mattress, and down sleeping bag. Our food would consist of standard car-camp fare for the nights with Ced and the jeep, but we also purchased packaged dinners and snack food for the overnights on the divide.

Another friend who wanted to help and follow along in his jeep was Dr. Gerald Coon. Jerry was the first president of the Ghost Town Club of Colorado, which we formed in 1958. Over the years we became great friends, making many jeep trips to high passes and ghost towns around the state. Because he was a medical doctor, I asked Jerry's opinion on proper foods to take along for maximum energy efficiency. He suggested a number of items which are standard fare for climbers and hikers today — dried fruits, nuts, and candy. He also designed a special concoction for us to drink in case we found ourselves in need of fast energy on the high ridges. It was a mix consisting of cocoa, safflower oil, honey, and powdered protein added to a bit of water. The idea is to use foods which require minimal digestive energy, yet deliver fast nutrition.

Communication between climbers and the drivers below would be an important factor, so we planned to use CB radios. I would carry a one-watt walkie-talkie and Ced would drive my jeep with a regular mobile unit.

We felt that our preparations were complete as Ced and I drove to Leadville via Mosquito Pass. At 13,188 feet, this is the highest continuously drivable pass in Colorado. We arrived at the summit just in time for sunset colors above the Sawatch Range to the west. It was a beautiful view with hundreds of emerald-like points of mercury vapor light spread out below in the city of Leadville. We camped that evening alongside Colorado 91 just north of Leadville on the way to Climax and Fremont Pass.

Friday dawned absolutely clear and, after some breakfast, Ced and I headed for Fremont Pass. Hugh was waiting for us right on schedule and we began loading our packs. Because the first portion of our hike took us through Climax Molybdenum property, we had to sign waivers of responsibility at the mine office in the event we should get hurt. As we proceeded on foot, Ced drove back to Leadville, over Mosquito Pass, and up the old Platte Gulch jeep

Ron Ruhoff (left) and Hugh Mayes begin the first section of their divide hike atop Fremont Pass, July 1963. Note the old town of Climax in the background, now gone. Cedric Damewood

road toward Wheeler Lake on the east side of the divide, in order to make radio contact with us near our planned camp atop Hoosier Pass.

As Hugh and I climbed up the west ridge of McNamee Peak, I learned how well-versed he was in botany. He collected wildflower specimens in little plastic bags and rattled off the technical names of every blossom and weed all the way up the ridge. Figworts, phloxes, saxifrage, and crowfoots were new names to me, but applied to many of the familiar alpine wildflowers. It was fascinating to learn new things about these colorful residents of the tundra from one who was working part-time at the Denver Museum of Natural History. Hugh claimed to have found several new and unrecorded species along our climbing route.

Once atop McNamee Peak, we were, at last, following the high ridges and views in all directions were magnificent. Clinton Peak was not far off and we soon were atop its 13,853-foot summit amid a variety of television translator equipment used to feed Denver stations to Leadville and Climax. Climax was still a town in 1963, and at that time it boasted the highest U.S. Post Office atop

11,320-foot Fremont Pass. The pass was named after explorer John C. Fremont, although it is doubtful that he crossed this portion of the divide during his travels in this part of the Rockies in 1844.

When we reached the midpoint between Clinton Peak and Point C (called Wheeler Peak on the newer maps), we made our first radio contact with Ced, who was below in Platte Gulch. We didn't talk long, because clouds had built up and we were getting corona discharge off the tip of the CB antenna. This condition makes a loud noise in the receiver, making communication almost impossible. The clouds didn't look that dangerous, but we could plainly hear the crackle of discharge off the antenna's tip even with the radio turned off.

Static discharge is a fascinating phenomenon, but one which all climbers and hikers must heed as a possible prelude to dangerous lightning. It may seem like fun to have your hair stand on end, feel prickles of static on your skin, have sparks fly off your camera as it hangs around your neck, or listen to the rocks buzz loudly, but one must know that extreme danger is pending. It is a must to get off the high ridges when these conditions begin to occur. Every year people are killed by lightning, not only on mountaintops, but at seemingly tame places like golf courses. Most of these accidents could have been prevented if the victims had been more safety conscious and kept an eye on the approaching weather.

Hugh and I arrived atop Point C, a high, prominent peak of large rocks about noon and enjoyed the view while having lunch. With the approach of threatening clouds, we prepared to drop below the ridges. The ridge that heads east from Point C toward North Star Mountain was our first real obstacle, as portions of it are sheer and jagged. As we skirted south around it, it proved just as well that we were off the ridge. A storm arrived with heavy rain and close lightning while we holed up in a rocky corner, safely sheltered. While we waited, the mountains and canyon reverberated with the magnificent sounds of thunder. To me, this is one of the most beautiful sounds of nature — truly "music of the mountains" and it can be thoroughly enjoyed if one has taken the precautions to wait in a relatively safe place.

As is often the case, the storm lasted only a short time, and before long, we were back on the divide ridge again with excellent weather all the way to Hoosier Pass. As we descended the last grades to the pass, we again talked to Ced on the radio and found that he was at the Hoosier Pass Campground making friends with the Luett family from Grand Island, Nebraska. Ced filled them in on our hiking project and reported to us by radio that they would have a pot of hot soup ready for us when we arrived!

While making our last steps down the ridge, our eyes were often glued to distant Grays and Torreys peaks far to the north. Our fifty-mile destination, Loveland Pass, was beyond those lofty summits and we knew our goal would be difficult to accomplish in four days. We arrived at camp about 6:00 PM, joining Ced and the Luetts. The soup was ready and a delicious treat after the strenuous day on the divide. Jerry Coon arrived shortly after we did and we all spent an enjoyable evening by a warm campfire discussing our travels. Needless to say, we slept well that night after completing our first section of the divide on schedule.

On the morning of the second day, we were given a sendoff by Ced, Jerry, and the Luetts as we headed up Hoosier Ridge toward Red Peak. The weather was generally clear and we enjoyed fine views of South Park and Mount Silverheels to the southeast. Silverheels has a high, rounded summit and stands out separately from the range near Fairplay. Its name came from a legendary dance hall girl who helped many people during a smallpox epidemic and then mysteriously disappeared, never to be seen again. Some say she caught the disease herself and no longer wanted to be seen.

Looking west, we could see North Star and Clinton peaks and towering 14,265-foot Quandary Peak in the Ten Mile Range. As we continued our hike that weekend, and on subsequent climbs, it was always fun to look back at peaks already climbed and miles already trod.

We made radio contact with our drivers as we neared the middle of Hoosier Ridge. They had driven over to Como, partway up the Boreas Pass road, and then up the Deadwood Gulch and Tarryall Creek jeep roads, where we could plainly see them far below.

Red Peak's 13,213-foot summit yielded at noon and we stopped for lunch and views of distant country. My photographs show a large valley around the old town of Dillon where Dillon Reservoir now lies. Breckenridge and the Ten Mile Range were also visible, but without the mountainside scars of the large ski area.

Ron Ruhoff rests atop Red Peak and looks north toward Breckenridge and Dillon. Dillon Reservoir was not yet completed in this 1963 photo.
Hugh Mayes

Hugh always went downgrade at a fast hop — sort of a jumping run. I followed his example all too often, as my knees later regretted. As we hopped off the north side of Red Peak, we suddenly came upon a hugh buck who was lazily napping on the ridge. He was as surprised as we were and I can vividly recall him jumping up with a loud snort and, showing the whites of his eyes, bounding away at a fast pace. It all happened too quickly to get cameras ready, but it was a sight I will never forget.

When we arrived at the old Denver, South Park & Pacific Railroad station atop Boreas Pass, Ced and Jerry were waiting for us. Also with them were Fred and Helen Giesel and their two boys, Steve and Eric. Ced knew Fred as a fellow employee of the *Rocky Mountain News* and had invited them to meet us that day while en route to the San Juans to do some four-wheeling. We didn't realize at the time that the Giesels would become future friends and take part in upcoming divide climbs.

After meeting everyone and talking awhile, Hugh and I decided to pack our overnight gear and head up Mount Baldy in the few hours of remaining daylight. The drivers went down the road to Baker's Tank to camp for the night, while Hugh and I climbed

Ron and Hugh meet the Giesels, Ced, and Jerry Coon atop Boreas Pass for supplies. The old Denver, South Park & Pacific Railroad station still stands. Bald Mountain is in the background. Cedric Damewood

slowly up the ridge toward Mount Baldy. We finally decided on a campsite in a 13,000-foot saddle just east of Baldy's 13,694-foot summit. This camp proved to be one of the most unique and beautiful of the entire divide hike.

Hugh and I set about making dinner and talked to friends below on the CB. After first boiling water for tea, we cooked two packages of freeze-dry Armour Star chicken stew. After boiling the stew for a long time, we found that it would not cook to tenderness — the water could not get hot enough at that high elevation. We finally ate the entire thing right out of the pan while it was boiling.

The sunset colors were beautiful to watch that evening from our high vantage point. Wispy, pink and purple clouds held close to distant peaks while others floated over South Park. We could see most of the climbing route followed so far as well as that portion of the divide we would follow the next day. Pikes Peak glowed warmly to the east above the vast valley of South Park. I took several photographs and then we set about getting sleeping bags ready. The wind had become quite strong and the task of getting ground cloth, air mattress, and sleeping bag down without them blowing off the mountain was difficult. I finally had to pin everything down with rocks, climb inside, then blow up the air mattress while lying down.

We spent a comfortable and restful night on that high saddle and woke to one of the most colorful sunrises I have ever witnessed. South Park was entirely filled with a sea of clouds with only Pikes Peak showing its summit above. The sun was just beginning to rise above the horizon and was bathing the clouds with rich golden hues. Mount Guyot looked like an inverted waterfall with clouds rolling upward along its eastern side and then dissipating in the sky. I used up a lot of film that morning, even before getting out of the sleeping bag.

As we got up, prepared breakfast, and readied our packs, the clouds kept increasing in size and getting nearer. We were convinced that we were in for a bad day as the clouds finally covered everything and left us standing in dense fog. Then, suddenly, a whoosh of wind came up and dissipated the clouds completely, leaving absolutely clear weather the rest of the day.

We started hiking and soon reached the south summit of Bald Mountain, which is the highest of its twin summits, and then continued down the divide ridge toward French Pass. At last radio contact, we knew our driving companions were on their way around to Georgia Pass, our next meeting place. By now it was very obvious that we would not make Loveland Pass on this particular trip. We were both tired and my knees were getting difficult to live with on the downgrades. When we reached French Pass, we found faint evidence of a road and jeep tracks. Ced had told us of his experiences in driving all the way over this pass a few years earlier. Miners had used this route for their wagons in the late 1800s.

When we reached the reddish, cindercone peak just south of Mount Guyot, we made radio contact with Georgia Pass and stopped for rest and lunch. I was still getting along fine on the upgrades and we soon accomplished the ridge to the 13,370-foot top of Mount Guyot. The mountain was named after a geologist by the name of A. H. Guyot, whose name has also been applied to underwater seamounts found in the Pacific Ocean. At the top we found a large cairn of rocks topped with an aluminum bucket whose bottom had been completely melted away by lightning strikes. This bucket would become an important part of a later chapter of this story. From our vantage point, we could plainly see

Ron Ruhoff stands atop Mount Guyot in 1963 near the old aluminum bucket, which later became a focal point for Uncle Dudley's story. Hugh Mayes

how far off Grays and Torreys still were. They would have to wait for another time. The intricate windings and ups and downs of the divide ridge take much longer to follow than one might think!

The climb down the long, steep north ridge of Mount Guyot was very slow and painful for my knees. It should have taken no more than a half an hour, but ended up requiring three hours! I even climbed down backwards at times, trying to relieve those sore "down muscles." We finally reached the pass just as the sun was setting and met Ced and his jeep. He drove us down to the campsite on Michigan Creek. The others were all there and Helen Giesel had cooked a huge pot of rice pelov for dinner. What a delicious meal! From that time on, the Giesels became the most wonderful of friends and that campsite has retained the name "Pelov Park" to this day.

During dinner that evening, we sat around the campfire and discussed our travels. Although Hugh and I still had another day off, we knew we were too tired to continue the hike. We had learned much about the problems involved in following the great divide ridge, but felt that we had accomplished much even if only half the distance we had set out to do. We were certain that our twenty-five miles on the high ridge was a much more difficult hike than many who had completed a full fifty in flat country. We had begun an exciting new challenge and I knew I would be back for more.

Georgia Pass to Argentine Pass, August 1971

Incredibly, seven years passed before my hiking project continued! During the intervening years, I climbed numerous mountains, backpacked into many corners of Colorado, and gained a wife and a daughter, but finding companions who were interested in the divide was difficult. Finally, Fred Giesel, who we had met on the first hike, was becoming interested in mountain climbing. We climbed Mount Sneffels together in 1970 and began talking about the long-neglected divide project. Early in 1971, Fred invited us to his home to make plans. Included were Uncle Dudley, Roger DeVries, and my Evergreen neighbor, Jay Popp, Jr., who was then a senior in high school. We spent the evening pouring over maps and made plans to continue from Georgia Pass to Loveland Pass, our original destination.

Jay, my wife Pam, two-year-old Christi, our dog Napoleon, and I left home on Thursday, August 5, 1971, with Bronco and tent trailer, heading for Michigan Creek Campground near Jefferson. The sun was just setting as we arrived and set up camp. Ced was already there, waiting by a warm campfire and the Giesels pulled in shortly thereafter. Roger would join us the next evening, as he had to work on Friday.

Friday morning dawned clear and, after breakfast and breaking camp, we all drove up to Georgia Pass, leaving the trailer in camp for Pam to pick up on the way down. Jay, Fred, and I were the hikers for the day and we spent some time taking pictures of each other with Mount Guyot in the background. I well remembered that gruelling climb down the ridge with my sore knees in 1963. Soon, we were hiking the divide toward Glacier Peak, reaching its 12,863-foot summit by noon. Mount of the Holy Cross was plainly visible far to the west and I recalled reaching its 14,005-foot summit in 1964. Dillon Reservoir sparkled down in the valley of the Blue

River, a new sight to us on the divide as it was not yet completed in 1963.

From atop Glacier Peak, we made radio contact with Helen and Pam, who were still at the Michigan Campground. They would soon drive over Kenosha Pass and up the Hall Valley road to set up camp near Handcart Gulch.

As we left Glacier Peak and headed for its eastern summit, we nearly stepped on a ptarmigan chick who was hiding in the grass. The little bird was separated from its mother and other chicks, as we finally spotted them some distance away. Ptarmigan have unique, feathered feet and camouflage coloring which makes them nearly impossible to see until right upon them.

Two more hours of hiking brought us to the top of 13,074-foot Whale Peak, where we had a fine view of Gibson Lake below on the Lake Fork of the North Fork of the South Platte River. Whale Peak was our lunch stop and while trying to raise our friends on the CB, we ended up talking to some folks who were boating on Lake Dillon.

At 3:30 in the afternoon, we came to a point on the ridge listed as USLM Bullion. This location brought into view the head of Hall Valley and we immediately spotted Ced's red jeep and Pam and Helen in the Bronco. We made radio contact and they reported that they planned to explore the old Whale Mine while watching us circle the ridge at the head of the canyon.

Looking west from atop Bullion Point, we could plainly see the jeep road which comes up from the ghost town of Swandyke on the Middle Fork of the Swan River. We had driven this road several years before while visiting Swandyke with the Giesels. The road is extremely steep and hazardous as it climbs to the divide ridge from where one can eventually follow the Deer Creek road down to Montezuma.

As we circled the Whale Mine, Pam and Helen drove back to camp to begin supper preparations. Ced drove up the Handcart Gulch road with the intention of picking us up atop Webster Pass, which would be our dropoff point for the day. Storms threatened for awhile as we approached the old Handcart Pass trail crossing the divide, but finally rumbled off giving no trouble. The Handcart Pass trail crosses between the Teller Mountain ridge and Handcart Peak and, according to Ced, was an early pack trail used prior to the construction of Webster Pass.

We made Handcart Peak by 6:00 PM and still had one more annoying little hill to cross before the last downhill to Webster Pass and our ride. As we crossed this section we tried to raise Ced on the CB, thinking he would surely be atop the pass by now. As soon as we topped the final hill, we could be Webster Pass clearly below, but no jeep. Just then we heard Ced calling on the radio and learned that he was stopped far down the valley by a large bog. Talk about a letdown! This meant another three miles of hiking before we could ride to camp and enjoy dinner. By that time, it was 9:30 and were we tired and hungry!

Saturday morning found us changing plans. We had intended to go back to Webster Pass and continue where we left off, but the bog was an obstacle we didn't want to tackle. We decided to drive north to Argentine Pass and work our way south. We had noticed a bulldozer parked by the bog and we figured that perhaps someone would have it cleared by the end of the day.

Argentine Pass, at 13,207 feet, is the highest drivable pass in Colorado; however, one can only go to the top from the east side. The western portion is totally impassable due to rockslides. Mosquito Pass, 13,188 feet, is still the highest continuous road in the state, although it is not on the continental divide. Argentine Pass once carried wagons between Peru Creek and Georgetown.

The old town of Waldorf just east of the pass was an extremely busy place around the turn of the century and once boasted the highest post office in the United States. In 1905, the Argentine Central Railroad was built to serve the mines of the Waldorf area and it even laid rails to near the crest of 13,587-foot Mount McClellan to carry tourists to the top of the highest adhesion railroad in the country. Views of Grays and Torreys peaks are magnificent from this grade, which one can easily negotiate with a four-wheel-drive. Shay locomotives were used extensively on the railroad's 7% grades. Engines of the same kind are still in use today on the Georgetown Loop Railroad. Unfortunately, the Argentine Central went broke and was torn out in 1928. Among other reasons for its failure, the builder, Edward J. Wilcox, was a Methodist minister who would not allow the trains to operate on Sundays, the best tourist day of the week. Practically nothing remains of Waldorf to remind visitors of its fascinating past, but it is an easy drive from Georgetown and the views from Argentine Pass and Mount McClellan are very worthwhile.

After saying goodbyes to our drivers, I began my divide hike again, this time with Fred and Roger, as Jay decided that he would rather drive than hike. We made the 13,738-foot summmit of Argentine Peak by 2:00 PM and, shortly thereafter, passed the high power line which feeds the Denver area from Public Service Company's Shoshone Plant in Glenwood Canyon. Built in 1915, this was one of the earliest such lines anywhere in the country. It crosses the continental divide three times between Glenwood and Denver — Hagerman, Fremont, and Argentine passes.

At 3:15, we reached the low point between Argentine Pass and Decatur Mountain and stopped to prepare some lunch. We included some of Jerry Coon's high-energy mix, concocted on our first hike. As usual, it did the job to help us along. Napoleon, our poolie dog, had some dog food and continued his exploring. He loved making the hike with us and must have walked four times as far as the rest of us with all of his explorations. From our lunch stop vantage point, we had a fine view of Shelf Lake below and watched some people riding horses on the ledge above the water.

We reached Decatur Mountain at 4:30 and talked to the others by radio. They were in Geneva Creek Canyon, somewhere near Smelter Gulch, heading for the Sill Mine at the end of the road, our evening meeting point. Another hour of hiking brought us to Revenue Mountain at 12,889 feet, and then soon to Silver Mountain. Snowbanks still covered many of the roads below us, and the drivers were having difficulty finding the proper route. We could easily see the entire area and guided them by radio to the proper roads. While doing so, Roger discovered that he had forgotten his canteen back on Revenue Mountain, so he walked back to get it while Fred and I enjoyed the views.

When Roger returned, the jeeps had reached the Sill Mine and we continued hiking to the saddle between Silver and Santa Fe peaks. Descending down a very steep couloir filled with loose scree, Napoleon became terrified and refused to budge. I had to carry him down and we finally arrived at the mine about dusk.

Sunday would be the finishing link between Webster Pass and the Santa Fe-Silver saddle. We decided that we could winch our way through the bog if necessary on the way up Webster Pass.

Before packing up the tent trailer, I asked Napoleon if he was ready to hike with us again. He understood perfectly, ducked his head, and walked right into the tent! After his experience on the scree slope, he had quite enough divide hiking and that was that!

When we arrived at the bog, we discovered that the bulldozer had indeed cleared it and we had no trouble driving to Webster Pass. This was the first time we had ever driven to the top via the east side, as it had been closed for many years by a large slide. Those four-wheelers who did cross, used the treacherous Red Cone route.

Handcart Gulch is a very beautiful place due to its large iron deposits. The entire canyon is full of iron springs, green moss, and stained rocks that make interesting photographic subjects. Above this scene rises the brilliant red and orange peak of Red Cone, which is 12,800 feet high and reminds one of the well-known Red Mountains near Silverton in the San Juans.

Legend has it that a rare breed of Brook trout, known as ironfish, live in the streams of Handcart Gulch. The iron-rich water has caused the fish to evolve with skeletons of nearly pure calcium ferrite. When fishing for them, it is only necessary to put a small horseshoe magnet on the line rather than a hook. Some of the nearby residents claim that fishing is best around the first part of April. I've always wanted to give it a try, but haven't found the time over the years.

We arrived atop Webster Pass about 11:00 AM and began the climb toward Landslide Peak. We came to a 13,214-foot high point prior to Landslide and decided to have lunch. The views from this spot were magnificent in all directions. Our 360-degree panorama included Torreys and Grays peaks, Argentine Pass, Square Top Peak, Geneva Park, Mount Evans, Kenosha Pass, South Park, Mount Silverheels, Mount Guyot, Bald Mountain, Quandary Peak, Mount of the Holy Cross, the Gore Range, Montezuma, and the road to Saints John. Times like this made the divide hike most fascinating, because we always enjoyed looking back at places we had been and looking forward to those yet ahead of us. We photographed these scenes constantly and also spent time taking pictures of alpine wildflowers and cloud formations.

Atop Landslide Peak, we were rewarded with great views of Geneva Basin and the road leading to the Sill Mine. Plodding on, we crossed Geneva Peak, Sullivan Mountain, and Santa Fe Peak. Santa Fe Peak offers fine views of the town of Montezuma and the road leading to the ghost town of Saints John. We crossed the mining road which comes up the divide ridge from Montezuma and made radio contact with Pam who had driven around to Peru Creek. We then dropped off the north side of the ridge into Warden Gulch where a jeep road comes up the main Peru Creek road. We started down from the same point on the saddle where we had descended east toward the Sill Mine on the previous day.

We met Pam on the road about 7:30 PM and completed the day at the King's Derby in Idaho Springs with some tremendous hamburgers. We had now completed the divide from Fremont Pass to Argentine Pass and were enthusiastic about finally reaching Grays and Torreys peaks and Loveland Pass when continuing the following year.

Argentine Pass to Citadel Peak, August 1972

The year 1972 found us all ambitious to continue where we had left off. Our son, James, was born in April and would later become a fine climber and backpacker himself. It had been nine years since Hugh and I hoped to reach Loveland Pass on the divide, but this summer would finally see our original fifty-mile hike completed.

Fred Giesel called a meeting at his home in early August and we found that several additional friends would be along this year. Ced joined us in planning, but would no longer be able to drive due to his failing eyesight. Roger De Vries and Jay Popp would be along as before and Fred's sons, Eric and Steve, both planned to hike. We would also have Jerry Gard and Mark Bonomo along for their first divide hike. Jerry was an architectural photographer and Mark was nearing completion of his goal of climbing all of Colorado's fourteeners.

Everyone wanted to hike rather than drive the first day, so we split into two climbing groups, driving a vehicle to each end of the hike, Argentine and Loveland passes. We would pass in the middle, swap car keys, and drive the other vehicle back to camp, which was planned at Pass Lake atop Loveland Pass.

On Friday, August 11, 1972, Jay and I met the others in Idaho Springs. I took Jay, Steve, and Jerry in my Bronco to Loveland Pass, while Fred drove his Scout with Eric, Mark, and Roger to Argentine Pass to begin the climb. My group arrived atop Loveland and set out along the ridge about 8:30 AM. Fred's party got started from Argentine Pass about 9:30. When we reached the 12,915-foot high point above Loveland, Jay decided to go back as he was not feeling well. He had just gotten over an illness and the altitude did not agree with him.

We soon found the location of old Irwin Pass which Ced had told us to look for. In 1867, Richard Irwin planned a pass across the divide at this location coming up from Grizzly Gulch. It never worked out and we could see how obviously difficult it would have been.

Jerry, Steve, and I topped Grizzly Peak about noon and had lunch consisting of crackers, cheese, and pepperoni. From here, we made our first radio contact with Fred's group, who were then going up the east ridge of Grays Peak. This was my second climb of Grizzly, having made a winter climb by the same route with Mike Sadusky back in 1959. The views are excellent from this 13,427-foot summit, especially that of Chihuahua Gulch Lake and the jagged ridge which separates it from the Arapaho Basin Ski Area. We all signed the Colorado Mountain Club register atop Grizzly and then headed down the long dip toward Torreys Peak.

The long, steep, west ridge of Torreys is a good example of a climb which is made easier by using a special breathing technique. I have used the rest-step system over the years, a breathing synchronized with steps. By picking a pace that is right and matching breaths with each step, the climb becomes much easier. Once a climber gets used to this method, it comes naturally and is much like shifting gears in a vehicle, depending on the grade. I have seen too many climbers move at too fast a pace and then have to spend much time resting to catch up on breath. With the right pace and rhythm breathing, one can go considerable distances without a stop.

Our group reached the top of Torreys Peak at 3:30 PM and met Fred and Roger there. We had already passed Mark and Eric partway down the slope and had given both aspirin for their headaches. We took pictures of one another and got the keys to the Scout before Fred and Roger continued on toward Loveland

Pass. Jerry, Steve, and I stayed atop the peak for a bit longer for some snacks. We watched the build-up of storm clouds approaching Grays Peak and I set up the walkie-talkie to monitor for static buildup. It soon came and we headed down the ridge toward Grays. We had gotten in the habit of using the CB for this purpose after learning that the extreme sensitivity of the radio could actually warn of static building up prior to a danger level when lightning strikes might be imminent.

When we got to the saddle between the two fourteeners, the weather looked quite threatening. We sat awhile, looking it over, and decided that since all three of us had already climbed Grays, we would bypass it in the interest of safety. We headed straight around the north side of Grays on the same contour as the saddle, eventually coming to the popular hiking trail. Here, we stopped to wait out some rain under our ponchos. Jerry fell asleep while we waited nearly an hour. We heard a number of close lightning strikes near the top of Grays, making us glad that we were not there. During all of this, the CB indicated practically no corona discharge, meaning our position was a safe one.

The rain and clouds finally went their way and we headed back to the divide ridge, about a quarter-mile east of Grays'summit. So far, this was the only place we had left the actual ridge except near Point C on the first day in 1963, but we knew there would be others in the miles ahead.

While together atop Torreys, everyone in Fred's group had said that they felt sorry for us because we had the rough Grays-Edwards ridge to do at the end of the day. It was rough, but Jerry and I thought is was delightful climbing because of the fascinating appearance and good rock.

Steve was getting very tired and had slowed down considerably. We took pictures of each other on the ridges prior to Mount Edwards and also of the low sun through the clouds behind Grays and Torreys. We found many beautiful orange lichens on the rocks to photograph in this area. The rich color of the late afternoon sun made them very photogenic. The views into Stevens Gulch and of Mount Kelso were wonderful and we could pick out the spot on the Mount McClellan ridge where the Argentine Central Railroad once terminated.

It was 7:30 PM before Jerry and I reached Mount Edwards'

13,850-foot summit. Steve skirted around its top to save the climb. From all along the ridge we had easily seen the Scout parked atop Argentine Pass. Once past Edwards, we figured it would be an easy walk. This proved quite deceiving however, as the distance from the peak to the pass is about a mile and took some time.

Halfway between the peak and the pass, we met a man who was camped on the ridge in a little rock shelter he had built. We talked awhile and learned he was doing a hike similar to ours. He had started from Mount Evans and was hiking the ridge to Mount Bierstadt, Guanella Pass, and Squaretop Mountain, and the divide to Loveland Pass.

As we approached Argentine Pass, we kept watching the lingering sunset which kept on and on and on in ever-darkening hues of red and orange. Nearing the pass, darkness set in, so I lit a chemical lightstick and used its bright, greenish light to see the way. These lightsticks last about four hours before slowly fading out and are an excellent source of emergency light to carry in a pack. We finally arrived at the Scout at 9:15 PM, noticing how red all the stars and distant lights of Denver looked through eyes accustomed to green light.

By the time we drove around to Loveland Pass, it was 11:30 and the others had just started out to look for us, thinking we might have had car trouble. Fred's party had also gotten down late, reaching their pass the same time we had gotten to ours. We drove over to little Pass Lake, just south of the Loveland Pass parking area and set up camp. Jay and I fixed a Lipton dinner and Fred fried up some hamburgers for the rest of the group. I had a bottle of wine which was shared by all. It had been a long, but beautiful day on the divide.

We all got up Saturday morning and felt pretty good despite the previous long day. Jay and I prepared our overnight packs for the next section of the hike. Fred had about decided to call it quits, but he too felt much improved over the previous night and decided to continue as well. As Jay photographed us heading up the ridge, we finally felt we were getting somewhere. At last, we had completed the original fifty miles and were continuing on.

Clouds and occasional light rain were already present by the time we topped a 12,752-foot point and headed for the next saddle. The radio indicated no static, but we holed up under ponchos until the sun came out. When we resumed hiking, we made radio contact with Steve in the Scout and learned that they would not be able to drive up a road above Loveland Basin to meet us. The road had been built for work on the Straight Creek highway tunnel and was now closed. The tunnel was originally named for Straight Creek Canyon on its west side, but, of course, is known today as the Eisenhower-Johnson Tunnel.

We finally reached that road atop the ridge late in the afternoon. We were directly above the tunnel at this point and noticed several large iron pipes in the ground. We surmised that they might have been test bores for the tunnel. There was also a large snow fence here to prevent slides into Loveland Basin. We could easily see both portals from here and the new highway being built down in Straight Creek Canyon. There appeared to be an asphalt plant smoking furiously in the canyon which gave us the answer to why we had seen smoke polluting the sky the day before as we climbed Grizzly and Grays peaks.

Our intentions were to head for the last dip in the ridge just south of Hagar Mountain to camp because there was a large snow-bank there for a water supply. We had located this spot with binoculars from Loveland Pass that morning. We arrived there about 5:30 amid threatening clouds and the distant sounds of thunder, and despite a lengthy debate about dropping to a lower elevation, pitched our tents as planned.

Luckily, the weather cleared and we cooked prepackaged turkey tetrazinni and beef stroganoff dinners. Hot soup and tea helped quench the thirst of another long day. The views of the sunset were beautiful that evening and we again took many pictures. We made a final goodnight call to our drivers at Pass Lake and found we could see each others' flashlight signals.

Sunday morning dawned a brilliantly clear day. After breakfast of hot tea and Tang, an instant breakfast, and another Teakettle dinner, we were on our way toward Hagar Mountain. We realized on this trip that Hagar is not the jagged, twin-peaked mountain seen so plainly from Loveland Pass, as we had always supposed, but a high point south of it. The jagged peak is frequently called "The Citadel," although the U.S.G.S. maps do not list that name.

We reached the summit of Hagar at 9:45 and found a Kodak film can with a very short pencil and paper inside. Three people

Roger DeVries (left) and Ron Ruhoff pause atop the 13,195-foot summit of Hagar Mountain north of Loveland Pass in 1971. The Ten Mile Range rises in the distance. Fred Giesel

had signed it and dated it simply "August 29." We added our names and spent some time taking pictures of one another atop its rocky summit. This made for some of the most spectacular "climbing the divide" photos we took. We viewed the Citadel from here and wondered if it would be as difficult to climb as it appears from Loveland Pass.

The Citadel turned out to be an easy climb from the southwest. Its western summit was a jumble of rocks which barely held all of our group of five while eating lunch. The ridge north of Citadel was something else again. We looked it over during our lunch break and knew we were in for some difficult climbing, especially with overnight packs. We worked our way past several steep sections and continued on to the low point between Citadel and peak 13,418. Here, we came to an abrupt forty-foot drop that we could not attempt safely without rope and hardware. There was absolutely no way around on either side — the ridge dropped away steeply in all directions. We had to go back! We elected to return to the saddle between Hagar and Citadel and descend west into Bobtail Canyon and down to the Jones Pass road.

We got back to the saddle by 2:30 and had some snacks before heading down a long scree slope. The upper slopes were indeed delightful scree, but lower, larger talus made for slow and steep going. At the bottom, we stopped at a pretty little alpine lake which still had an iceberg in it. We made cherry and grape snowcones and refilled canteens with fresh, cold water — a luxury no longer available without purification procedures.

With so many photographers in the group, self-timer photos of everyone seated on the rocky shores of the lake were mandatory before continuing down through the meadows of Bobtail Creek. We could plainly see the Jones Pass road ahead as it came over the divide and soon made CB contact with Steve and Jay, telling them of our change in plans and asking them to meet us at the old Bobtail Mine instead. They spent a long time searching for us with binoculars before finally spotting us, even though we could easily see them on the road. Soon, we came to a trail leading to the mine. Along the way, we saw much evidence of the elk herds I knew to be in the area.

With about a half mile to go, Fred, who had already lost his wallet somewhere on the Citadel ridge, discovered that he had left his camera on a log at our last stop. Poor Fred! It wasn't his day! Fred and Roger left their packs and returned for it while Jerry, Mark, and I continued on to the mine. When they rejoined us, we packed up and drove to Idaho Springs for another fine dinner at the King's Derby. We had now completed fifty-six miles of the divide ridge.

Citadel Peak to Vasquez Pass, August 1973

For the third year in a row, we continued our hike along the divide in the month of August. Fred and Eric Giesel, Ced Damewood, Roger DeVries, Mark Bonomo, Jay Popp, Jerry Gard, Jerry's son Bruce, and I were all at a planning session at Fred's house. We planned to make up the lost section from Jones Pass south to the cliff on the Citadel, then overnight from Jones Pass north to Berthoud Pass.

I left home in my Bronco on Thursday evening, August 2, 1973. Everyone was driving separately and planned to meet at the Bobtail Mine. I reached the top of Jones Pass just after sunset and stopped to enjoy the view of city lights to the east and a clear sky full of bright stars. Dvorak's "New World" Symphony was on the radio and I got out of the Bronco for a few minutes to enjoy the sight and sound.

We were all up early on Friday and fixed some breakfast before driving to the top of Jones Pass. Soon, we were on our way south toward Pettingel Peak and the Citadel. A helicopter flew over the ridge very close to us just south of the pass. The crew spotted us, hovered momentarily, and waved. They were surveyors for the Denver Water Board, which operates the diversion tunnel under the divide beneath Jones Pass.

Mark was always a fast hiker and kept well ahead of the rest of us all day. When we arrived atop Pettingel, he had already spent an hour on the summit. We stayed another hour, having lunch and snowcones and enjoying the views. The weather was excellent, although some scattered storms appeared in the distance. Pettingel's 13,553-foot summit is a very prominent one and offers a superb vantage point with wonderful views in all directions. We could see our destination to the south — the jagged north ridge of the Citadel and even the little lake at the head of Bobtail Creek. To the east, the Henderson Mine and the crater of Red Mountain were visible. That huge crater makes the mountain look like a volcano, but it is the result of the "glory-holing" method of mining molybdenum ore. We had seen this crater from distant Landslide Peak two years earlier and recalled being alarmed by the appearance until we finally realized what it was.

On our way again, we reached the low point on the ridge just north of the Citadel at 3:30 PM. Jerry, Roger, and I went on to the base of the cliff that had stopped us the year before, while the others began the descent into the valley. I examined the cliff, finding that it would not have been difficult to climb up to the point where we had given up, but decided that the loss of twenty feet or so of horizontal measurement on the divide was not worth risking the climb back down without a rope.

While we were taking pictures of the cliff and the many beautiful alpine flowers in the area, we saw the others far below us, approaching the valley. The clouds began to envelope the ridges above us and made interesting photographic subjects. Many of these pictures helped fill in the storm sequence of Richard Strauss's

"Alpine Symphony," a slide presentation I performed in concert with the Colorado Philharmonic Orchestra a few years later in Evergreen.

We reached camp at the Bobtail Mine and settled down to a fine chili dinner which Roger DeVries had supplied for us. We all enjoyed the fire, some good wine, and a discussion of the day's climb.

On Saturday, we left with overnight packs and started across the Vasquez Mountains for our Berthoud Pass destination. Jay would keep in radio contact with us and pick us up on Sunday. The big climb of the day was the west ridge of Vasquez Peak. It required some energy food and careful pacing and breathing. On the way, we met a lone porcupine, making a continental divide hike of his own, and heard, but didn't see, a flock of sheep grazing below in Vasquez Creek Canyon.

All the time, I was aware of the buildup of threatening clouds in the west. I got to the top of 12,947-foot Vasquez Peak at 1:45 with the others about twenty minutes behind me and Mark already ahead on the next high point. I talked to Jay via radio and learned that he had just photographed us by telephoto from his position on Jones Pass. The weather was obviously heading our way and I told everyone to be prepared to drop off the ridge.

The clouds wasted no time closing in on us and, as we descended to the low point east of Vasquez Peak, static began to show on the CB. We dropped off the ridge some distance and had lunch while waiting out what would prove to be only the first storm of a frustrating day. When the sky cleared for a time, we regrouped with Mark just east of a 12,900-foot point. This was the spot we had originally planned for our overnight camp, but more static and rain once again forced us off the ridge. This time we were forced to stay under shelter for over two hours as lightning flashed and thunder boomed all around us. I passed the time by looking at the many tiny alpine flowers nearby under my poncho and finally used my pack for a pillow and took a nap.

Eventually, the rain and lightning let up and we headed back to the saddle. There was still some static in the air, however, and the weather showed little sign of clearing. Reluctantly, we dropped off Vasquez Pass and had Jay pick us up. Clear weather on Sunday would have permitted a short hike to our goal of Berthoud Pass, but as it turned out, Sunday was another day of the same stormy weather, so we made the right decision by aborting the hike.

Rollins Pass to Arapaho Pass, August 1976

After that wet and rainy descent down Vasquez Pass, three years passed before I was able to again accomplish a significant divide hike. Our group had attempted the Rollins-Berthoud section in 1974, but had made only two miles before being chased off by a severe, long-lasting storm. In 1975, I was occupied with a new daughter, Anna, and could not join Fred, Jerry, and Roger when they made a successful hike from Rollins to Berthoud. Now, in the Colorado Centennial year of 1976, Fred and I drove separate vehicles to the town of Eldora and then continued west to Buckingham Campground. Mark joined us there as planned and we left two vehicles at the campground and drove around toward Rollins Pass in Fred's Scout. We camped near Yankee Doodle Lake and discussed plans for the next day's hike.

Saturday dawned bright and clear and, after breakfast, we drove up the abandoned railroad grade to Rollins Pass. Roger De-Vries met us there and we began the hike north with overnight packs. We passed the site of the old Corona railroad station. One now finds only piles of weathered boards strewn about this broad, flat area where once snowsheds completely covered the station and the trackage of the wye. Inside, out of the weather, a station, telegraph office, and restaurant were located. The Denver & Salt Lake Railroad was a standard gauge line which operated across the continental divide prior to the construction of the Moffat Tunnel. Keeping the railroad open across the pass during the winter months was an unbelievable task. Old photographs show the many difficulties of snow fighting operations.

The hike north from the pass was generally easy going and the weather was clear with a brisk westerly wind. The views over the east side toward King, Betty, and Bob lakes were spectacular and as usual, we took many photos. We arrived at Devil's Thumb Pass about noon and stopped for over an hour to enjoy lunch, snow-cones, and the views. Devil's Thumb rock towers above the pass to the north and is a plainly visible landmark from Middle Park

Roger, Fred, and Mark stand above King Lake near Rollins Pass. Ron Ruhoff

Mark Bonomo scrambles along the actual divide ridge just north of Rollins Pass. Mount Neva and the Arapaho Peaks are in the distance. Ron Ruhoff

Devil's Thumb, Devil's Thumb Lake, and the divide hikers on Devil's Thumb Pass all made it into this photo. Ron Ruhoff

near Tabernash. A little cony visited us and of course tried to beg some handouts during the lunch hour. These tiny alpine members of the rabbit family are also known as pikas.

We noticed the build-up of heavy clouds to the west and were soon on our way over the next hump on the ridge. Predictably, the weather got nasty and we dropped down the east side of the divide to a small lake, about a quarter-mile north of Devil's Thumb. Rain fell and we waited under ponchos for about an hour while lightning crashed up on the ridge. The echoing thunder was magnificent. I didn't have a CB along because we had no driver below, but I did have a small AM-FM radio which served the same purpose as a static indicator. Even during the heaviest lightning, there was no indication of corona discharge at our location.

By the time the rain stopped, it was 5:00 PM and we elected to set up tents on the alpine grass just east of the lake. The temperature dropped to a nippy 39° and, having become somewhat chilled while waiting in the rain, I crawled into my sleeping bag to warm up. Fred and Roger did the same and while we all rested warm and dry in our tents, more rain and much wind pelted us. Finally, we got the stove going and boiled water for hot soup and dinner.

The weather eventually cleared somewhat and we saw a beautiful sunset red in the sky over the ridge above us. The moon was just rising over the lights of Denver in the distance. Those thousands of sparkling emeralds, the city's mercury vapor lights, and the bright full moon made a wonderful sight. I took some time exposures of our tents lit by candle lanterns with the city lights behind them. We went to sleep in real comfort about 9:00 PM with the temperature holding at 40°.

Sunday morning arrived with overcast skies and cold wind. The fare for breakfast was scrambled eggs and coffee. After packing, Mark and I hiked back to the point on the ridge where we had dropped off the day before. Fred was feeling poorly, and, considering the weather, decided to head down. Roger joined him and they headed down to Jasper Lake with plans for me to pick them up at Hessie that afternoon after I reached my car.

Mark and I continued along the divide and reached a 12,923-foot high point with a Colorado Mountain Club register proclaiming it Jasper Peak. While we signed it, we were visited by a weasel, who darted about the rocks peaking out at the intruding strangers. The weather was clearing and views in all directions were beautiful. The entire Middle Park area and Granby Reservoir spread out to the west. Byers and St. Louis peaks and the distant Gore Range stood out sharply on the horizon. To the east, Upper and Lower Diamond Lakes sparkled below.

We reached Mount Neva's 12,814-foot summit about noon and stopped for lunch. The jagged Indian Peaks rose to the north beyond Lake Dorothy and two unnamed lakes still full of icebergs sparkled below. Once more, clouds were building in the west and we hurried on to tackle the rugged north ridges of Mount Neva. With heavy overnight packs, we were forced to skirt a portion of its western side. Halfway to Arapaho Pass, we were forced off the ridge by a shortlived but furious thunderstorm. The wind was so strong and gusty that my poncho wouldn't behave at all and I got quite wet. Once the storm blew through, we reached Arapaho Pass and made the trail descent to Buckingham Campground and our cars.

I drove over to Hessie as planned and found Fred and Roger had been waiting for only a little over an hour. We drove back to Rollins Pass to retrieve the other vehicles and continued home via

Tolland. Another fine section of the divide had been completed, but I had to make plans to complete the two missing sections — Vasquez to Berthoud and Berthoud to Rollins — in order to complete 100 miles.

Berthoud Pass to Vasquez Pass, September 1977

I chose the first weekend of September 1977 to attempt the Rollins to Berthoud section once again. Roger and Dori DeVries joined me, and we began at the site of the old aircraft beacon near Berthoud Pass where our 1974 hike was cut short by a storm. Parking Roger's Scout near the beacon's concrete pad, we backpacked north toward James Peak in perfectly clear weather.

Our views to the west included Middle Park, completely filled with fog, and the sparkling Arapaho Lakes on the east side. These lakes are similar to hundreds of other alpine lakes that are set into glacial cirques along the eastern side of the Rockies. These blue-green jewels are remnants of the ice age when the prevailing westerly winds piled snow to sufficient depth to form glaciers on the mountain ridges. The giant glaciers gouged out the granite to leave impressive east faces on the mountains and natural dams of glacial moraine which contain the alpine lakes.

Roger, Dori, and I made a lunch stop at the 12,110-foot point from where we could look down upon the Crater Lakes. They were glittering like diamonds as the sun reflected off windblown ripples of water. Looking northeast, we could plainly see the Needle's Eye Tunnel on Rollins Pass.

As usual, clouds were building rapidly in the west as we continued south from our lunch break. When we reached the point we estimated to be directly above the Moffat Tunnel, we knew that we would have to get off the ridge once again. We descended to a little alpine pond near the Iceberg Lakes and spent nearly two hours under ponchos, wishing the rain would go somewhere else. It did not go away, so we hiked lower to a flat grassy area near another pond to set up camp for the night. Another hour of rain delayed pitching the tents and the temperature dropped to 40°.

Sunday morning dawned clear, but rapidly deteriorated. Soon, James Peak was a terrible mass of heavy gray clouds. Stumped again, we headed back to the Scout. Before we could reach it, rain, hail, and lightning played all around and we had to drop low again and allow the storm to pass before we could safely reach the Scout which was parked on a dangerous promontory. We ended up driving back to Rollins Pass in heavy rain. This elusive section of the divide would, again, have to await another time.

It seemed a shame to let another year go by with so little accomplished, so we decided to try the section between Vasquez and Berthoud passes before the year was out. We met on Saturday, September 24, but Friday found the first snow of the season blanketing the high country. We left a vehicle at the foot of the Vasquez Pass trail on the Henderson Mine road, and then went on to Berthoud Pass, finding a sparkling clear day with five inches of fresh snow covering everything. Hot coffee and rolls from the Berthoud Pass restaurant provided a welcome delay before beginning our hike.

Fresh snow gave the divide ridges an entirely different appearance than that to which we were accustomed, but it was a beautiful photogenic day. The wind was strong and cold and kept us in parkas and gloves most of the day. After passing the ski lift equipment, we reached the first high point and then continued on to Stanley Mountain, the highest summit of the day. From there, it was a long, steep descent to Vasquez Pass where we picked up the old Vasquez Trail which we had traveled in 1973.

Before going down, we stopped to enjoy the view and, for the first time that day were able to enjoy the warmth of the sun with no wind. We could hear the drone from the Henderson Mine ventilators and see many points along the divide that were familiar to us from previous hikes. Jones Pass, Pettingel Peak, Red Mountain with its glory hole, and Clear Creek Canyon were plainly visible. Personally, I had now completed eighty-five miles of the divide ridge and only needed the Berthoud to Rollins section to make my one hundred.

Uncle Dudley's Day

Over the many years of our divide hiking experience, Cedric Damewood, also known to us as "Uncle Dudley," was one of our most enthusiastic followers. He was involved in much of the planning and drove for us during our first two hiking sections. Ced participated in planning for later trips, although he was no longer able to drive due to failing eyesight. Finally, in 1974, he moved to California to live with his daughter, Cleone van Westen. While there, Ced kept in contact with us and sent many taped voice letters which contained numerous stories about his life and jeeping adventures in Colorado.

Shortly before moving west, Ced became obsessed with a unique idea for the day he would inevitably pass on. He always remembered my first trip on the divide with Hugh Mayes and the great difficulty I had getting down from Mount Guyot with sore knees. Ced came up with a plan for having his ashes scattered over his favorite portion of Colorado around Georgia Pass. He recalled my description of the old aluminum bucket atop the summit cairn of Mount Guyot that had been severely melted by lightning strikes. Ced felt that the bucket should be replaced with a new one and that, when it was carried to the mountaintop, it would offer him the opportunity for a "free ride."

Ced, Fred Giesel, and I discussed the idea over the years and Fred and I assured Ced that his wishes would be carried out when the time came. Ced wanted to have an enjoyable get-together for all involved, hoping that several members of his beloved Mile-Hi Jeep Club and the Ghost Town Club of Colorado would be present. He envisioned a large group of people parked atop Georgia Pass watching those climbing to the top of Mount Guyot with the bucket.

Ced gave great thought about who might preside over the ceremony, but the folks he had in mind passed away themselves during the intervening years. Finally, I suggested to Ced that he make a tape recording for the occasion that we could play atop Georgia Pass. He liked the idea and proceeded to make the tape, entitled "Sermon on the Mount," which he sent to me sometime during 1977.

Cedric passed away in the spring of 1980 at an age well over eighty. His daughter Cleone contacted me to set up plans for a summer day when everyone could go to Georgia Pass. Notices were posted in the various club newsletters and all of his friends were told that Saturday, July 26, 1980, would be "Uncle Dudley's Day."

Cedric Damewood, "Uncle Dudley," with his faithful jeep and favorite pipe pauses for a photo while driving for the divide hikers. Ron Ruhoff

Cedric Damewood,
1898-1980.

Ron Ruhoff

My family and I arrived at Michigan Creek Campground on Friday evening, meeting the Giesels and Van Westens there. The next morning, we were joined by members of the jeep and ghost town clubs and we all headed for Georgia Pass. The climbers were Fred and Eric Giesel, Roger DeVries, Ed and Marlene Zimmerman, Hal Harnagel, and I. Cleone placed the box containing Cedric's ashes in a shiny, galvanized bucket and I tied it to my pack. We all began the climb and arrived atop the peak at 10:30 AM. I had a small cassette with me to play a copy of Ced's tape on the summit at the same time those below listened to theirs. Ced's message contained a tremendous amount of history of the area and vivid descriptions of the views one gets from atop Georgia Pass even though he had been blind and away from Colorado for several years.

After the message was played, I threw the ashes out over the mountainside with help from a brisk wind and placed the new bucket atop the summit cairn. The climb back down to the pass took only thirty-four minutes, quite a difference from that gruelling three hours in 1963! Everyone gathered for lunch at Michigan Creek Campground and, as Ced had wanted, had a grand time.

Berthoud Pass to Rollins Pass, September 1980

The events of Uncle Dudley's day prompted me to make another try for the Berthoud to Rollins section. Hopefully, the third time would be the charm that would complete my 100 miles. Ironically, this section is the closest to Denver and is the very view I get from I-70 at Genesee Park as I drive home to Evergreen each morning from my night job in Denver. I can name off each peak by memory — Mines, Flora, Witter, Eva, Parry, Bancroft, and James. I had become acquainted with new climbing companions from Evergreen, and Joe Cook, Jim Karuzas, and Sid Phillips all agreed to join me. We left in two vehicles on Friday afternoon September 12, 1980 and drove over Berthoud Pass, stopping for supper in Winter Park. From there, we drove to the old railroad wye near Riflesight Notch on the Rollins Pass road to make camp. We slept well and awoke to clear skies and much frost on the tents. After oatmeal and coffee, we packed our overnight gear for the two-day hike.

Uncle Dudley's Sermon on the Mount

Hi folks. Welcome aboard. We've had in mind a number of better speakers, but we've postponed the date for this gathering over the years, and they kept falling by the wayside. Finally, my young associate in Denver, Ron Ruhoff, told me that if I wanted anything said, I'd have to do it myself. It's rather unusual to be asked to preach your own funeral sermon, but then, we're unusual people.

First, I'd better touch briefly on why we're here. A number of years ago, when Ron Ruhoff was hiking the divide, he stood on the top of Mount Guyot while we were on Georgia Pass with the jeeps. He found an aluminum kettle on the cairn up there that had been hit by lightning so many times that it was in bad shape. He promised that someday he'd go back with a receptacle in better condition. It occurred to me that this was an opportunity for a free ride. Since he'd have to climb the peak to put a new container on top, why not put my ashes in it, carry them to the top, sprinkle the ashes, and leave the container. And so, here we are.

Also from Georgia Pass we have a seat here on the fifty-yard line, from which we can watch the mountain climbers scaling the peak. Guyot is spelled Guyot, but we people who speak English have so much trouble with French, we call it Gheeoh. This peak looks like a pyramid. Moveover, you don't have to come here to climb it to see it because it's visible for miles and miles in all directions — whether you're forty miles down into South Park or from the valleys of the Snake, or the Swan, or the Blue, or even the highway up by Frisco. And if, in succeeding years, anybody remembers Uncle Dudley, all they have to do is look up and there's the monument, or peak or whatever that represents Uncle Dudley.

I realize you people have to get home, while I'm not going anywhere and I'm in no hurry. I could talk endlessly, but I'll have to close and in so doing I recite the last verse of William Cullen Bryant's poem "Thanatopsis."

My friends, farewell.

We first drove up the old Rogers Pass road and left Joe's truck at a point below where I had left off three years earlier with Roger and Dori. We then drove my Bronco back to Berthoud Pass to begin. We followed the zig-zag maintenance road to the top of Colorado Mines Peak and then continued north to Mount Flora and Mount Eva. While we rested and ate lunch atop Mount Eva, Jim made a quick jog over to the top of Witter Peak, which is not on the actual divide ridge. I had already climbed it once before from Chinns Lake, so let Jim take that one on his own.

Mid-afternoon found us atop the highest point of this section of the divide, 13,331-foot Parry Peak. Upslope weather conditions had changed the wind direction from west to easterly and some fog was swirling about the peaks. As we crossed the ridge to Bancroft Peak, the mists began to obscure the ridges behind us. Once atop Bancroft, we could see the saddle between Bancroft and James, but could not locate anything close to the description of the nice campsite Fred, Roger, and Jerry had raved about on their 1975 hike of this section.

We could see only jumbles of large rocks and we scattered as we climbed down toward the low point of the saddle, trying to locate the elusive, grassy shelf. Finally, we discovered it while climbing toward James. It was hidden behind a large rock outcropping, but they were right. It was a beautiful, grassy alpine shelf, just large enough for the four of us to set up camp. The shelf was the only possible place around and it offered a terrific view of Ice Lake directly below. There was no running water nearby, but a short walk up to a snowbank sufficed.

Once back to camp with fresh water, I fired up the Primus and proceeded to make hot tea and a freeze-dry dinner. While waiting for the water to boil, I listened to a recording of the Brahms Violin Concerto on my little FM radio. It blended in perfectly with the swirling clouds and distant views. I couldn't help but think, "Wouldn't Brahms or any of the other famous 18th and 19th century composers be amazed to realize how and where people of the future would listen to their music."

The clouds had completely circled the tops of Bancroft and Parry as we set up camp. The mists would at times shoot up past us and then break into swirls and eddies as they caught air currents above the ridge. Occasionally, direct sunlight illuminated the clouds

Joe Cook enjoys the serenity of the shelf camp above Ice Lake with Mount Bancroft in the background. Ron Ruhoff

Ron Ruhoff enjoys the sounds of a full orchestra on his small FM radio while enjoying colorful cloud formations from a camp above Ice Lake. Ron Ruhoff

Jim Karuzas (left) and Joe Cook enjoy a morning view of Ice Lake and the eastern plains from the shelf camp near James Peak. Ron Ruhoff

or nearby cliffs. I began photographing this view as the beauty of it all increased. As the sunset color began to warm and redden, tufts of reddish clouds clung to Bancroft and Parry and a large, orange cumulus cloud towered to the south with a brilliant new moon above it. The shadows of James Peak stood out sharply on the mists rising above Loch Lomond. As the color faded, the lights of Denver and the sparkling moon took over.

We woke Sunday to light in the east, but no color as the eastern horizon was completely clouded over. Once the sun topped the clouds, however, we had brilliantly clear weather for the remainder of the day. Breakfast consisted of coffee, oatmeal, granola bars and some of Joe's over-abundant supply of fresh eggs and sausage which he shared with everyone.

We reached the summit of James Peak at 9:30, making my fourth climb of this 13,294-foot mountain. My first climb was in winter in 1957. The view from the top is wonderful, especially looking down the precipitous east face toward Little Echo and James Peak lakes. To the west were the Gore Range, Mount of the Holy Cross, Mount Massive, and Mount Elbert. We could plainly see nearly all of the summits we had crossed in our many years of divide hiking. With the 100-mile goal nearly accomplished, a poignant feeling accompanied those views as I thought of the many good times and troubles we had covering those high ridges. To the north, Longs Peak and the Arapahos had fresh snow on their summits and we could see Rogers Pass where this hike would terminate.

As we descended the north ridge of James, we encountered a long series of tricky, jagged rocks and then crossed the old Ute Trail, used by Indians long ago. Haystack Mountain to the east really did look like one, and we had a fine view of Heart Lake and both portals of the Moffat Tunnel as well as the Needle's Eye Tunnel and Yankee Doodle Lake on the Rollins Pass Road.

At Rogers Pass, we found an old water flume dug out of the hillside beginning at the divide ridge and heading around the corner toward the old railroad grade. Perhaps it was used to supply water for trains or the Corona Station, or it may have been some trans-mountain diversion ditch. Rogers Pass is drivable from the west, but there is only a trail on its eastern side.

At 1:15 PM we reached the point where I had left the ridge with Roger and Dori, thus finally filling in all of the gaps in the hike between Fremont and Arapaho passes. The one hundred miles was, at last, complete. True, I still had 572 miles to go to complete the entire divide in Colorado as some other climbers have done, but the amount I accomplished will remain an unforgettable experience.

As I compiled information for this book, I found that the section I have covered measures out to only 94.2 miles, but considering the fact that we had to hike all those hypotenuses rather than the measured distance on the maps, I am convinced I filled out a full one hundred!

Perhaps there is a lot of repetition in this story of driving to and from meeting points, descriptions of the views and the ups and downs of the hikes, but I hope it will give those who have yet to try such a hike some helpful hints. Hiking along the continental divide ridge has been a fascinating experience and I sincerely hope that those who try it for themselves will have as much fun as we have had. ▲

Kathryn, Mary, and Wes Mauz, Jr. scale the east ridge of Grizzly Peak near Loveland Pass. Wes Mauz

Part III

Hikers Who Have Completed Colorado's Divide

Carl and Robert Melzer, Julius Johnson, 1936

When Hugh and I first dreamed up our idea of divide hiking, we were not aware that it had been done before. Over the years, I had heard from various climbers who "thought" it had been done, but it was not until I began talking to veteran mountaineer Carl Blaurock that I learned of the remarkable journeys of the Melzer family.

Carl said, "Well of course it's been done! Carl Melzer and his boy Bobby did the whole thing back in 1936. Then Carl's grandson did it again in 1976."

This news opened up a whole new source of information for me and I met with Dr. Robert Melzer early in 1987 to learn more about his experiences. Carl Melzer led the very first Colorado continental divide expedition and was accompanied by his eight-year-old son, Robert, and Julius Johnson, a nineteen-year-old college student. Carl was a Denver school teacher at the time and had the summer off. He kept impeccable journals of the entire trip and photographed it not only in 35mm black and white and Kodachrome, but also in 16mm movies. His story was published in the August 6, 1938 issue of *The Saturday Evening Post* and featured Carl's color photography — the first time color was used in the magazine.

Carl Melzer first got the idea for such a hike in 1920, when he looked down on the Colorado high country from an airplane. He was so impressed with the view of the hundreds of high mountain peaks, he told himself that someday he would climb every one of them. The divide hike began on July 6, 1936 at the Wyoming border near the Whiskey Park Ranger Station and ended near Chama, New Mexico, sixty-four days later. The trio logged a total distance of 768 miles in fifty-four hiking days. (That distance included side trips to campsites, adding almost 100 miles to the

Young Bob and Carl Melzer sit atop Mount Zirkel in 1936.
Dr. Robert Melzer Collection

divide's length as recorded in the appendix.) They averaged an impressive fourteen miles per day.

Weather was a constant problem that summer, dishing out above average amounts of rain, snow, hail, and lightning along the high ridges. They had numerous experiences with static electricity, lightning bolts, and the smell of ozone in the air. How did they keep dry? They didn't, but kept on nevertheless with ambition and determination rarely found these days.

Those of us who climb in today's world of nylon, freeze-dry, Goretex, plastic, and all the other lightweight equipment can only marvel at the methods used in 1936! Clothing was very primitive by current standards: leather jackets, jeans, wool shirts, baseball caps, and composition sole hunting boots. Lady's rubber raincoats were the only waterproof protection used. Carl and Julius used early eight-pound down sleeping bags, while Bob had a nine-pound kapok bag. They did not use tents at all, but covered their bags with the rubber raincoats during wet weather in an attempt to keep dry. Young Bob didn't complain one bit and loved it all except for the times the mosquitos were insufferable. He was highly allergic to their bites and had some miserable moments, including an eye that was swollen shut for awhile.

Carl Melzer, Bob Melzer, and Julius Johnson (left to right) relax near Chama, New Mexico, at the end of their epic divide journey in 1936.
Dr. Robert Melzer Collection

Mrs. Grace Melzer drove for the climbers, meeting them at prearranged passes every five to seven days with food supplies and clean clothing. Their records show a total of 299 pounds of food consumed which included: hard tack, 28 pounds; sugar, 28 pounds; grapenuts cereal, 20 pounds; oatmeal, 1 pound; chocolate bars, 21 pounds; cheese, 25 pounds; shelled nuts, 38 pounds; tunafish, 16 pounds; bacon, 3 pounds; dried beef, 3 pounds; and dried milk, 24 pounds. There were no plastic bags available then, so food was kept in muslin sacks placed inside rubber bathing caps! Drinking water was taken freely from natural streams and snowbanks without the use of canteens or bottles and without the worry about the diseases we must be so careful about today. When the hike was completed, none of the three had lost a single pound. Bob had always suffered from bronchitis attacks, but during their hike and ever since he has not had another.

Carl Melzer devised a unique method of leaving a record of their presence atop mountain peaks and passes along the way. He prepared about 200 half-inch copper tubes, cut to a four-inch length and stamped with his initials and a serial number. Each contained a record of the date, location, weather information, and signatures

July 17, 1936
(Left) Julius Johnson indulges the camera atop Haystack Mountain.
(Center) Carl Melzer looks out from the summit of Haystack Mountain.
(Right) Young Bob Melzer with his "kit" atop Haystack Mountain.
Photographs from the Dr. Robert Melzer Collection

of the three climbers. The ends of the tubes were closed with rubber stoppers and each was placed among the rocks, much like the familiar Colorado Mountain Club registers. Melzer placed 117 tubes on their 1936 divide hike and another 51 the following year atop all of Colorado's fourteeners. Anyone stumbling onto one of these relics is encouraged to contact Dr. Robert Melzer or the Colorado Mountain Club.

Wildlife was abundant on the 1936 hike. The trio watched timber wolves stalk elk and saw so many deer that they grew tired of photographing them. Eagles followed the hikers for hours and grouse, ptarmigan, and sage hens were often underfoot. Coyotes howled every night from one end of Colorado to the other.

Once, during some extremely foggy weather while dropping off Mount Baldy toward Boreas Pass, the Melzer party followed the wrong ridge and ended up in Como in South Park. The Denver, South Park & Pacific Railroad, by then operating as part of the Colorado & Southern network, was still in operation across the pass between Como and Breckenridge. They boarded the train and rode back to the top of Boreas Pass where they spent the night in the depot-hotel with the train crews. Young Bob was sent to bed in an upstairs room so that the railroaders' off-color stories would not reach his ears. The railroad station still stands in dilapidated condition, but trains have not traveled the route since 1937.

Carl, Bob, and Julius reached the New Mexico line one day ahead of schedule. Not one of them suffered any sickness during the long trek. Only on the way home, after such an adventure, did Bob get carsick. A most remarkable mountain journey had been completed! As if that experience was not enough, the following year the same trio climbed all 51 Colorado fourteeners then recognized. Mount Shavano and Tabeguache Mountain completed the list on their 65th day of climbing after hiking 456 miles and driving 4211 miles.

Chuck Betcher, 1969

After the Melzers, the next Colorado divide hiker who I am aware of was Chuck Betcher of Aspen. Unable to locate him directly, I must rely on an article by Charlie Meyers in the September 30, 1969 *Denver Post*. Betcher made the first solo divide hike and even cached his own food supplies at fourteen passes ahead of time to make the trip completely self-sufficient. Beginning at the Wyoming line on July 3, he reached New Mexico eighty days later.

Betcher encountered bad weather, hunger from arriving late at his re-supply points, and a few understandable psychological difficulties with the lonely trip. He took extended rest periods in Aspen and Silverton, and somehow lost only one of his 140 pounds. He commented upon returning, "I never really cared for the city, but now I've actually come to hate it. But there was one aspect of civilization I have no complaints about — girls. I had forgotten how good they look! When I got back to Aspen, I almost blew my cool."

Douglas Barr and David Miller, 1971

In 1971, Douglas Barr, David Miller, and Allison Platt, all co-workers at the Keystone Ski Area, started south from Wyoming on the Fourth of July. Doug had come up with the idea of the hike while parked atop Hoosier Pass. "I realized that if I had my backpack on, I could follow the continental divide right on over to Fremont Pass. Then, I immediately thought, why not follow the whole thing?"

Dave Miller thought the idea was terrific and Allison Platt wanted to join the trek so that she could write a story about it. Doug's parents and several friends met them with supplies at seven passes, and the hikers stocked two other supply points ahead of time by filling five-gallon pickle barrels with food and caching them near an access point. As most hikers have commented, they always looked forward to meets with their suppliers and the "real meals" they could then enjoy. They carried some fresh food for the first day after each meet and had one discouraging accident when, shortly after leaving the supply team on Monarch Pass, Dave dropped a dozen eggs, breaking all but one.

The trio skirted the formidable Indian Peaks section by dropping west on the Buchanan Pass Trail, hiking past Monarch Lake, and rejoining the divide crest at Arapaho Pass. Allison decided to quit at Berthoud Pass after an impressive 209 miles. Doug and Dave continued on and at Independence Pass, they hitchhiked into Aspen for a planned midpoint rest. While there, they looked up Chuck Betcher, who was working in a mountaineering store, and compared notes on their respective adventures.

Continuing south, they encountered problems in the Cochetopa Hills due to low elevation and the indistinct wandering of the divide. Water was also a problem — very scarce and unreliable due to stock grazing in the area.

Near Wolf Creek Pass, Dave and Doug noticed some hot springs marked on the map on the West Fork of the San Juan River. They decided that a break from the divide was in order and the visit turned out to be "the definite highlight of the whole trip," according to Doug. "The things we missed the most were good food and hot showers." Once refreshed, the hikers continued south to the New Mexico border.

Dave and Doug remain active in outdoor sports. Doug has

Doug Barr enjoys a refreshing bath in the hot springs northwest of Wolf Creek Pass.

David Miller

Dave Miller looks out over Chihuahua Gulch and Lake just south of Grizzly Peak. Douglas Barr

taken up kayaking and followed most of the major river runs in Colorado during breaks from his schooling and job at the National Oceanic and Atmospheric Administration in Boulder. Dave loves skiing and operates a helicopter ski service in Jackson, Wyoming, during the winter and guides raft trips on the Snake River in the summer.

"It was the great expedition of my life," Dave recalled. "I was from Massachusetts, and when I came to Colorado I had this feeling that I wanted to know the mountains well and to understand how expansive they were. The divide hike was a great introduction to mountaineering, a wonderful alpine experience, and I learned a lot about the country.

"Thinking back on it all, I liked the San Juan Mountains the best. Weminuche Pass, in particular, had the most fantastic views. It is a very spirited place. I think the most unique spot on the divide ridge is "the Window" near Rio Grande Pyramid. That great notch in the ridge casts a ray of light across the country to the east at sunset. It was very evident why the Indians had spiritual feelings about that country."

Fort Carson Striders, 1972

A group of twenty-two army officers and enlisted men from Fort Carson, Colorado, completed the divide hike from Chama north to Wyoming in forty-nine days in 1972. Led by Major Harry Wicksell, Jr., the group began on July 3 and averaged twelve miles per day on their so-called "Stride-the-Divide" mission.

The ambitious exercise was actually a study of long-term affects of exertion at high altitudes. Along the way, they were met by a helicopter every four days with a new supply of C-rations and as much water as they could carry. Each meeting point meant hot meals, a change of clothes, and mail deliveries. How's that for logistical support? The Denver Post article of August 28, 1972 reporting the trip makes no mention of exact route, but notes that an average elevation of 11,000 feet was maintained.

The infantrymen were allowed to use either military issue packs or commercial equipment and not surprisingly, most agreed that the civilian packs proved superior to the government issue.

Three pack mules also made the trip, which would indicate that the group stayed away from the rugged peaks and ridges as much as possible.

When asked what one thinks about on such a long hike, one man replied, "Steaks, newspapers, hot showers, a thirty-day leave, and a banana split."

Eric and Tim Ryback, 1972

Eric and Tim Ryback's exploits near Colorado's continental divide in 1972 are recounted in his book, *The Ultimate Journey*. After hiking both the Appalachian and Pacific Coast trails, Eric planned to follow the divide from Glacier Park to the Mexican border — an awesome 3,000-mile undertaking. Tim dropped out after the Wyoming section, but Eric completed the trek solo. His route, however, was often a more general following of the divide and he skirted many of the higher peaks. One of Eric's goals was to promote the "Continental Divide Trail" and the U.S. Forest Service assisted him with his food drops on many occasions.

Tom and Judy Melzer, Jim Beblavi, 1976

Tom and Judy Melzer had been married only a year when the continental divide beckoned them to attempt a repeat of the 1936 adventure of Tom's father and grandfather. Although several friends and relatives accompanied them along short sections of the divide, finding another climber who could devote an entire summer to the trek was difficult. Finally, their longtime friend, Jim Beblavi, agreed to join them. The starting date was June 28, 1976, one day after Tom and Judy's first wedding anniversary.

The supply system worked much the same as in 1936. Tom and Jim's families drove to the access points with food and clothing needs. Prescheduled meeting points were: Rabbit Ears Pass, July 4; Willow Creek Pass, July 8; Milner Pass, July 12; Berthoud Pass, July 20; Loveland Pass, July 23; Hoosier Pass, July 28; Independence Pass, August 3; Monarch Pass, August 10; North Pass, August 13; Spring Creek Pass, August 17; Wolf Creek Pass, August 23; and

Chama, New Mexico, August 27. Each meet worked out on schedule and the trio feasted on pizza, milk shakes, watermelon, and other things that could not be carried on the hike. The longest section between supplies was the eight-day stretch through Rocky Mountain National Park and the Indian Peaks.

The weather was much more favorable than in 1936, although this group too had its share of rain in Rocky Mountain National Park and the San Juans. Modern ponchos, tents, and waterproof items made the going far more tolerable than that which the 1936 party had endured.

All three hikers were about twenty-three years old at the time and carried packs that weighed from forty-five to fifty pounds. No one experienced any sickness along the way except for the last several days when all three developed diarrhea from some unknown source. Checkups found no parasites, but it was a warning to be extremely careful with water supplies on such a venture.

Carl Melzer helped with the planning of the 1976 expedition, and per his suggestion, the trio completely avoided the Indian Peaks area by dropping west off Buchanan Pass and rejoining the divide at Arapaho Pass. The Three Apostles in the Sawatch Range were also skirted on the Timberline Trail around the south and west sides of those jagged summits. Other peaks were skirted as well, some in the interest of time or weather, and others to avoid ridges that were simply too rough to safely negotiate with overnight gear.

There were many painful moments for both Judy and Jim along much of the trip. During the first week, Judy suffered a stress fracture of her foot and had to endure considerable pain throughout the rest of the journey. She also sprained her wrist when she slipped on some wet rocks in Rocky Mountain National Park. Jim had a terrible time with sunburned hands, which became swollen and infected. Despite these hardships, their spirits remained high and the hike was completed on schedule. In fact, the planned meeting time near Chama was 9:00 AM and the hikers arrived at 9:05, while the rest of the family, driving cars, were twenty minutes late!

When all were together at the state line, a grand celebration was in order. Tom's father, Robert, and grandfather, Carl, were both there, as was the other veteran from the 1936 hike, Julius Johnson. It was a thrilling time for Carl Melzer to witness the successful completion of the divide by the third generation of the family. He

Tom Melzer, Judy Melzer, and Jim Beblavi still manage smiles atop Loveland Pass despite Judy's sprained wrist and Jim's sunburned hands.
Tom Melzer Collection

Julius Johnson, Carl Melzer, and Dr. Robert Melzer (left to right) join in a re-union near Chama, New Mexico, in 1976. Jim Beblavi

An elite group, from left to right, Carl Melzer, Judy Melzer, Tom Melzer, Jim Beblavi, Dr. Robert Melzer and Julius Johnson, celebrates the completion of the 1976 Melzer Continental Divide Expedition near Chama, New Mexico. Note that Carl is wearing the same hat and backpack that he used on his 1936 hike. Jim Beblavi Collection

had been on hand when the group left the Wyoming border and had remarked, "I just wish I could take enough Geritol and cortisone to do it all over again. Why heck, I'd give a million dollars to be able to do it all again!"

Referring to his own father, Tom noted that "one of the things that kept us all going was the thought that if an eight-year-old boy could do it in 1936, we could too!" Dr. Robert Melzer joined the group to hike several short sections, as did Jim's father, Carl Beblavi.

Judy observed, "When you end a trip like that it can go but one of two ways — divorce or marriage. We knew it was marriage!" Judy became the first woman to hike the entire divide in Colorado and, now that their children are reaching hiking age, they are giving serious consideration to taking them along on another such hike — the fourth generation of Melzers to do so. Tom and Judy agree, however, that the next time they would make the trip in sections at a more leisurely pace to allow time for more enjoyment of the country along the way.

I asked Tom, Judy, and Jim to relate some of their most vivid memories and highlights of the hike. Judy felt her greatest impressions were the many encounters with wildlife and the feeling of being in places that no person had seen before. "We saw numerous herds of elk," recalled Judy, sometimes over 100 head. We saw elk nursing and sometimes they were so curious that they would come right up to our camp. We saw a seven-point bull near McHenrys Notch and another was standing only fifty feet from our tent one morning. Once, we heard what we thought were birds chirping, but it turned out to be cow elk talking to one another. There were mountain goats on top of Grays Peak and I always enjoyed watching the little pikas scurrying among the rocks with tufts of grass in their mouths."

One of Judy's favorite stories is of crossing a high, rocky ridge in Rocky Mountain National Park. "We were traveling in a severe fog, which can be very disorienting. When we were certain that a steep drop-off existed only a few feet away, we began to crawl, not wanting to take any chances. The more we crawled, the more our imagination got the best of us. Suddenly, a wind came up and momentarily cleared the clouds. Much to our surprise, we found the drop-off to be only a gradual depression of no more than five feet. We really felt silly!"

One of Tom's most profound feelings came to him as they descended Bald Mountain toward Boreas Pass. "As we climbed down toward the pass, I realized that the abandoned building was the railroad depot that my father and grandfather had spent the night in with the railroad crew back in 1936."

Not long after the 1976 hike, Tom and Judy lived in Oregon for a time. They did some hiking there, but Tom remembers that "the mountains where we hiked in Oregon rarely got above timberline and we almost got claustrophobia hiking in the dense forest. We just ached to get up high into the open tundra where we could see out. We would occasionally see a tiny knob above timberline and hike up to it just for the view. We really missed the Colorado high country!"

Jim Beblavi had trouble with his sunburned hands and wore socks over them most of the time. When the trio reached Fremont Pass, Jim hitchhiked down to Leadville to buy cotton gloves, which proved a comfortable remedy. The man who drove him back up

Tom Melzer, Jim Beblavi, and Judy Melzer (left to right) gaze into New Mexico from the divide near Blue Lake. Tom Melzer Collection

the pass from Leadville turned out to be an Outward Bound instructor. Jim had gone through an Outward Bound course seven years before. His driver that day told him, "Your Outward Bound experience begins when you get on the bus to go home." Jim noted that his Outward Bound experience had indeed helped him in many ways on the divide as well as in other situations over the years.

Jim told of Judy and Tom meeting a man backpacking by himself near Weminuche Pass who enthusiastically told about his hike and the fact that he had been out for ten days. He then asked how long Judy and Tom had been hiking while being obviously proud of the fact that he had been out so long. Judy thought for a minute and then said, "Well, let's see, we came from the Wyoming border and have been hiking for fifty-five days now." The timing was perfect and the man's jaw must have dropped a foot!

Gary McKay, 1978

Toward late 1977, Gary McKay decided that he'd had enough of his high-pressure job as a travel agent and that he wanted to get away from it and do some traveling of his own. He had read Eric

Gary McKay writes in his journal after a long day on the divide. He is camped by Round Lake near Rabbit Ears Pass and is cooking potatoes left by another camper. Gary McKay

Ryback's book and become particularly enthused about making a long, solo backpack trip. "I really wanted to be alone for awhile, so decided to make a solo trip of it. I was twenty-eight years-old at the time and only weighed 130 pounds. I didn't feel that I had the stamina to do the entire divide from Canada to Mexico, so decided to try the Colorado portion first."

Gary decided to hike the divide from south to north, thinking that the southern mountains might have less snow early in the season. He began on June 12 somewhat east of the actual divide and followed the Cumbres & Toltec Scenic Railway to Cumbres Pass before turning north along the divide. With his early start, he still encountered considerable snow and progress was difficult at times. The San Juans remained his favorite section, however, because of the rugged and colorful scenery.

Food rations became a problem for Gary because he underestimated his food consumption. "I planned for only one packaged dinner each day, along with assorted granola, candy, and nuts, but I was hungry all the time. There were many times that I could have eaten two or even three dinners a day, but I had to get by with what I had. My funds were limited too, so it was not easy to buy more along the way."

Each large supply package was prepared, dated, and marked for a specific section of the divide. The supply points were usually taken care of by friends, but the first drop was made by a forest ranger at the Silver Falls Guard Station in the San Juans and one was mailed to the post office at Sargents. Gary recalled, "When I stopped at Sargents, I spent a good part of the day eating at the restaurant there. When I picked up my supplies at the post office, it was like getting a CARE package from home."

Friends met Gary at Tincup Pass and drove him to Buena Vista for dinner, ice cream, and a comfortable stay in a motel. Two more rest stops were made along the way at Leadville and Grand Lake. While in Leadville, he made a side trip to climb Mount Massive.

Just before his Grand Lake break, the food shortage became critical. "I camped beside the Colorado River that night and couldn't sleep at all. I kept fantasizing about big steak dinners. Finally, I got up about 5:00 AM and hiked to a store that opened at 8:00. I bought a cheesecake and ate the whole thing back at camp. I craved food so badly, I can't emphasize enough to others to be sure to take along more than you think you will need."

One evening, somewhere along the divide in the San Juans, Gary set up his camp, which consisted only of a ground cloth, pad, sleeping bag, and tarp, and walked to the top of a rise to photograph the sunset. As darkness approached, he turned to walk back to camp, but could not locate it. "It was a frightening feeling to realize that I had lost my bearings so close to camp. My equipment was so inconspicuous that it became easily hidden behind some bushes and everywhere began to look the same at dusk. I wandered around all night long, and never did find the spot until dawn. It really taught me a lesson to be careful about such things."

Gary's hike ended after ninety days on September 12, at Encampment Meadows, Wyoming. Gary found the source of a branch of the Encampment River trickling out of nowhere as a spring and as it increased in size, he followed it to the Wyoming border. When he arrived in Encampment, he had lost fifteen pounds from his normally thin frame. "My friends really kidded me about being so skinny, but I never felt better in my life. I felt really healthy.

"After completing the hike, I lived with some friends for awhile until getting my own place again. I just didn't feel like sleeping in the house and ended up camping in their backyard most of the time. I was so used to sleeping under the stars, watching for meteors and satellites, I didn't want to stop."

After ten years, would Gary like to do the divide again? "Yes, I'd really like to hike it all again. Remembering all the details of the hike, names and dates, is difficult, but I'll never forget the special feelings I had on those beautiful, high ridges. It was all such a wonderful experience! Next time, I'd want a partner though. I didn't mind being alone, but there were so many times when I'd see a beautiful sunset or scene and want to share it with someone."

Gary McKay lives in Arvada, Colorado, with his wife Ellen and two fine boys, all of whom love the experience of backpacking.

Doug and Ellen Stewart, 1978 and 1981

While Gary McKay was hiking north along the divide in 1978, Doug Stewart and Ellen Altemus left Encampment in early September and headed south. Neither party knew of the other until a chance meeting near Rabbit Ears Pass. When tracking down names of divide hikers, I managed to find both Gary and Doug and, for the first time, told each of the other's success.

Doug and Ellen shared the divide adventure from the Wyoming border to the middle of Rocky Mountain National Park, where they descended Flattop Mountain and got a ride into Estes Park. Ellen had to begin a new job and could not continue on the hike. They parted and Doug went back to the ridge to continue on his own. A short time later, when Doug was hiking near Arapaho Pass, he heard a voice shouting "Doug! Doug!" and there was Ellen, racing down the trail to greet him.

Doug recalled, "Ellen had gotten so homesick for the divide, that she came back on her free days and hiked seventeen miles one day all the way from Monarch Lake to Arapaho Pass and back down the Arapaho Creek trail until she found me. She accompanied me as far as James Peak before leaving to work again." I'm sure that Ellen was missing a certain hiker as well as the divide!

One of the highlights of Doug's adventure was his climb of Torreys Peak, the summit of which he reached just at sunset. The weather was fine, the views wonderful, and he decided to camp for the night atop the 14,267-foot summit. He made another mountaintop camp on the summit of Mount Guyot just before a supply meet with Ellen on Boreas Pass.

By the time Doug reached Marshall Pass, a heavy autumn snowstorm had made hiking nearly impossible and he realized that the remainder of the trip would have to wait for another year. As it turned out, three years passed before Doug and Ellen, by now married, returned to Marshall Pass in July 1981 to complete the hike south to New Mexico.

The Cochetopa Hills came first with their good and bad features. The hills offered a gentle and gradual start, allowing some time for acclimizing, but on the bad side was the lack of water and the poor trails. Gary McKay, in his brief conversation with them atop Rabbit Ears Pass three years before had forewarned them of these problems in the Cochetopas.

The "natural springs," which were shown on the map, turned out to be nothing but cattle wallows, and they had to hike waterless for some fifteen miles. Approaching San Luis Peak, a thunderstorm gave them quite a downpour, which was reassuring and welcome, but they had to lose a thousand feet of elevation just to stock up on water before they could continue along the ridge.

Doug and Ellen delighted in viewing the abundant wildlife. They saw pikas with tufts of grass in their mouths stop to watch them pass and heard the distant whistles of marmots warning each other of the two-legged intruders. Those high-pitched whistles seemed to alert deer and elk of their presence and the larger animals were often seen bounding off into the distance. Ptarmigan chicks would scatter at their feet before the hikers knew the birds were hidden in the grass.

Rio Grande Pyramid was a favorite mountain for Doug and Ellen and, having viewed it in the distance for so long while hiking the great San Juan loop, they delighted in climbing to its summit for the fine views of the San Juans in all directions. A wild strawberry patch profuse with delicious fruit was a highlight of the descent from the Pyramid to Weminuche Pass.

Doug and Ellen made their last camp exactly on the divide ridge near Chama Peak and viewed a colorful sunset as they looked southward to the last stretch of their hike to the New Mexico border. When they reached the state line the next day, they came upon a

Ellen and Doug Stewart pause near Twin Lakes in the San Juan Mountains
Doug Stewart

*Ellen Stewart
ponders a culinary delight
at a camp near
Chama Peak.*

Doug Stewart

sign that said, "Do Not Enter." When they read the opposite side of the sign, it said exactly the same thing! Yes, there is some private land along the divide near the border, but Doug and Ellen concluded their hike about two miles from the actual divide crossing at a spot their maps showed to be a state-owned wildlife refuge.

Relating some of his experiences on the divide, Doug commented, "The most profound thing was being completely alone for weeks on the first trip. I would go until dark, then set up my sleeping bag with no one around. I slept in the open as much as possible and loved the feel of the wind on my face during the night. Those nights atop Torreys and Guyot were my favorites. While I was looking for a bivouac spot near an unnamed peak south of Independence Pass, a mountain goat walked side by side with me for some distance. I always liked the high alpine country the best, but Ellen seemed to get more pleasure from the wooded valleys with their streams and wildflowers.

"After my article in *Empire Magazine* about the first trip, someone from the Colorado Mountain Club wrote an editorial condemning me for making such a hike alone, claiming that search and rescue parties 'get tired of that nonsense.' I wrote back, agreeing that I could have gotten into trouble, but that the challenge of taking care of myself was part of the experience. I really believe that an experienced hiker has the right to do it that way. I found that after about two weeks out, one gets 'tuned' to the outdoors in a way shorter trips could never do. You gain a level of self-sufficiency that you can't get with a horse or vehicle."

Doug and Ellen now make their home in Carbondale with their two young children. The little ones are learning to become hikers and all Stewarts love to return to their favorite spots along Colorado's continental divide.

Wes and Mary Mauz, 1971-1983

One of the most uniquely enjoyable methods of backcountry travel that has become popular in recent years is llama packing. These fascinating beasts of burden from South America are being raised and used as pack carriers in ever increasing numbers in the United States. They have become a favorite companion to many who love mountain trekking.

Wes and Mary Mauz of Golden, Colorado, got their first llama in 1984 and now keep over twenty at their foothills ranch for use in a llama packing business called Timberline Llamas, Inc. During the summer months, they offer pack trips along portions of the continental divide in the San Juans of Colorado and the Bridger Wilderness Area of Wyoming. The experience of camping far back in the wilderness has been opened up for many who cannot or would rather not carry their own packs. Some find the small, sturdy llama a more pleasant companion than the more common horse.

A llama can carry up to 100 pounds and will willingly follow just about anywhere a person can hike, except in rough boulder or talus areas. Wes says, "The llama will follow along just like a big puppy or dog or perhaps a porter or sherpa. They're really neat animals to be around. They not only carry the gear for our custom ers, but each person can have their own llama to walk with and take care of if they like." Timberline Llamas offers several scheduled pack trips each season.

For the Mauz family, the llama business was an outgrowth of their longtime love for the mountains and backpacking. After an extended five-day backpack, Wes got the idea of following the entire divide through Colorado and began the project with his wife Mary in 1971. It was a project that required a number of years because they were never able to devote an entire summer to hiking. The last leg of the divide was finally accomplished in 1983. As their children grew up, they too became involved in the project and, now in their late teens, Wes Jr. has only to complete Tennessee Pass to Boreas Pass and Kathryn lacks only the Independence Pass to Boreas section.

Wes explains their interest in the divide. "Everyone was doing all the fourteeners and we always liked trekking better than indi-vidual mountain climbs anyway. It seemed like something new and different to do."

Mary recalls their favorite section was from Wolf Creek Pass south to Chama. "It was so beautiful. We saw numerous waterfalls, mar-mots were curious and came right up to us without fear, and there were towering rock cairns, built long ago by sheepherders. One evening we heard a chorus of coyotes that rang out across the tundra. It was such a beautiful sound and they kept it up without

Kathryn, Mary, and Wes Mauz, Jr. show some of the fun of llama trekking at Lake Pass in the Sawatch Range. Wes Mauz

pause for nearly half an hour."

Wes loves all of their high country adventures and suggests to those who stay home that they should try a mountain trek, perhaps with a llama to carry the load. "Life," he says, "is a collection of experiences, but one needs to go out and collect them."

Chris and Mark Cole, Jon Tipps, 1987

One of the most unusual and daring adventures along Colorado's divide took place during the winter of 1986-87. Jon Tipps of Evergreen, Colorado, and Mark and Chris Cole, brothers from Jackson, Wyoming, made the first cross-country ski trip along the divide, beginning on December 15 at Chama, New Mexico, and ending in Encampment three months later on March 16.

Jon Tipps first got the idea for the trip when he was teaching at the Devils Thumb touring center and then got the Cole brothers to join in. All are expert skiers and Mark was also an instructor at the National Outdoor Leadership School as well as an emergency medical technician.

Equipment included metal-edged skis with loose heel bindings, double leather boots, tents, sleeping bags designed for minus forty-degree weather, extra skis, avalanche equipment, sleds to pull a portion of the load, and $300 worth of maps. Food was cached ahead of time in September and totaled more than 900 pounds.

Their route was faithful to the divide except for a major detour around the Front Range and Rocky Mountain National Park. They left the divide at Independence Pass and went straight north through Vail, along the Gore Range, and then picked up the divide again at Rabbit Ears Pass. They encountered some severe weather at Stony Pass in the San Juans and had to spend two days holed up in a snow cave. Many nights were mild enough to sleep out in the open, however.

One of their most enjoyable rest stops was at the Monarch Pass lodge, where they sat by a warm fire and watched the Super Bowl on television. After a week of twenty below zero weather in the Cochetopa Hills, the night spent in warm beds was a real luxury.

Mark, Chris, and Jon reached their pickup truck in Encampment after ninety-two days, and, despite their worrying about its starting, the truck roared to life immediately. Many questioned the wisdom of such a journey, but backcountry skiing can be safe if those who attempt it are properly educated and aware of the hazardous conditions and special skills required to deal with them.

(The account of this trip is from an article by Charlie Meyers in the *Denver Post* of March 19, 1987.)

▲

To date the list of those who have completed Colorado's continental divide is very short. It is not the sort of thing many people have been inspired or able to do. I have given an account of all such people that I have been able to learn about, but I don't doubt there are some I have inadvertently missed. If so, I would certainly like to hear from anyone who has completed Colorado's great divide. The divide offers a challenge unlike that of individual mountain climbs and, for those who are willing to "Go out and collect the experience", to quote Wes Mauz, the reward will be a lifetime of beautiful memories. ▲

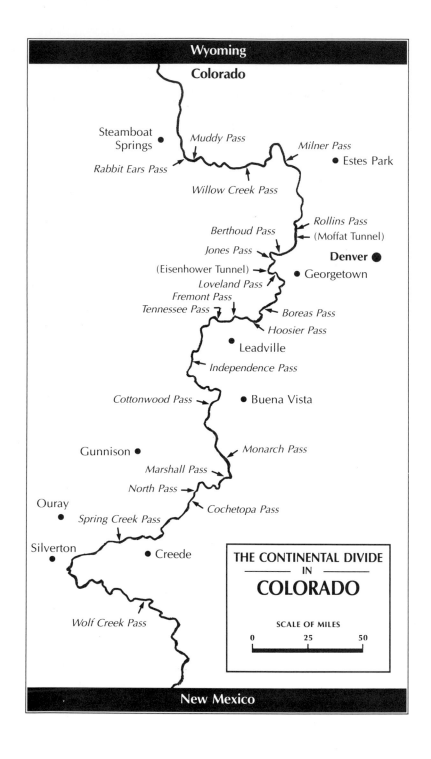

Wyoming

Colorado

Steamboat Springs

Muddy Pass

Milner Pass

Estes Park

Rabbit Ears Pass

Willow Creek Pass

Rollins Pass
(Moffat Tunnel)

Berthoud Pass

Jones Pass

Denver

(Eisenhower Tunnel)

Georgetown

Loveland Pass

Fremont Pass

Tennessee Pass

Boreas Pass

Hoosier Pass

Leadville

Independence Pass

Cottonwood Pass

Buena Vista

Gunnison

Monarch Pass

Marshall Pass

North Pass

Ouray

Cochetopa Pass

Spring Creek Pass

Silverton

Creede

THE CONTINENTAL DIVIDE
IN
COLORADO

SCALE OF MILES

0   25   50

Wolf Creek Pass

New Mexico

Part IV

A Guide to Colorado's Continental Divide

One of the first decisions to be made in planning a divide hike is on which end to begin. Most thru-hikers have traveled in a north to south direction, beginning at the Wyoming border. As Jim Behlavi pointed out, "Perhaps there is a psychological feeling that you're going downhill all the way as you go south, but we felt the most important reason for choosing this direction was the long, gentle start. You have about seventeen miles of gradual climbing to the first high point on Buck Mountain. At the New Mexico end, seven miles takes you right to 12,000 feet and you remain high for the entire San Juan area."

The following guide begins at the Wyoming border. Roads provide access to quite near the divide crossing of the Colorado-Wyoming border. Referring to the Routt National Forest map, follow the main road north from Steamboat Springs to Hahns Peak and Columbine. Continue north on Forest Service 550 to one mile south of the Wyoming border where Forest Service 412 leads east to a crossing of the divide. At the divide crossing of road 412, the Fireline Stock Trail can be followed with 4WD one-half-mile north to the state line. The 1976 Melzer party began their hike in this manner and built a rock cairn on the border to mark their starting point. It is also possible to reach the road 412 crossing of the divide from the east via Cowdrey, Pearl, Damfino Creek, and Hog Park.

The following description is grouped by the major passes which provide automobile access to the divide. The mileages in the headings are rounded to the nearest one-half-mile.

Wyoming Border   Mile 0

The first seventeen miles of the divide offer a very gentle beginning along the Fireline Stock Trail, which follows the actual ridge very faithfully as far as Buck Mountain. The Ellis Park jeep road provides access at mile 5.8 from Forest Service 550 north of Hahns Peak. This spot marks the northern boundary of the Mount Zirkel Wilderness Area.

Most hikers on the divide in late June encounter considerable snow near Mount Zirkel. This is a problem that has to be dealt with no matter which end of Colorado you begin, as the high country generally has a heavy snowpack until well into July. Mount Zirkel itself is very rugged and offers jagged ridges along the divide. With care, the mountain can be included on the hike with overnight packs. The 1976 Melzer party found numerous mosquitos in the area, but all who have traversed this wilderness claim it to be one of the most beautiful places in Colorado.

Buffalo Pass   Mile 54

The Buffalo Pass road is about four miles south of the southern Mount Zirkel Wilderness boundary and offers an easy dirt road access to the divide near Steamboat Springs. There is a campground atop the pass. The east side of the pass leading to North Park is quite steep and not in as good a condition as the road on the west. Prior to the construction of Rabbit Ears Pass, Buffalo Pass was the main route between North Park and Steamboat Springs.

Rabbit Ears Pass   Mile 69

The first paved highway crossing of the continental divide is reached at Rabbit Ears Pass, near where U.S. 40 descends into Steamboat Springs. Easy hiking and numerous lakes are encountered between Buffalo Pass and Rabbit Ears Pass. The pass was named for the twin rock outcroppings atop Rabbit Ears Peak, which somewhat resemble the ears of a rabbit and are visible for great distances. Only four miles of pleasant hiking lead to the next crossing of U.S. 40 at Muddy Pass with Baker Mountain being the high point in between.

Muddy Pass   Mile 73

The highway at Muddy Pass offers the lowest crossing of the divide in Colorado at 8,772 feet. John C. Fremont crossed this pass in 1844 and its name was derived from nearby Muddy Creek. Routt National Forest ends here and a section of private ranch land must be skirted as the divide heads east into the Rabbit Ears Range. The Stewart and Melzer parties both walked several miles of Colorado 14 north from Muddy Pass, skirting private property, before joining the divide again near Arapaho Pass.

A short distance beyond the old Arapaho Pass crossing at Mile 83, national forest land begins again and the divide follows the boundary between Routt and Arapaho national forests all the way to Rocky Mountain National Park. Arapaho Pass itself is a primitive road which passes through both private and B.L.M. land.

It is thirty-one miles from Arapaho Pass to the next highway crossing at Willow Creek. Along the way, a primitive road crosses the divide at Troublesome Pass, and an abandoned fire lookout still stands on the top of 12,296-foot Parkview Mountain. Many logging roads criss-cross the divide ridge along the Rabbit Ears Range. This area is one of the lowest sections of the divide in Colorado, and those who have hiked it suggest carrying adequate water, as it can be difficult to find in this low, wooded country.

Willow Creek Pass   Mile 113.5

Colorado 125 crosses Willow Creek Pass and was first constructed as a roadway from an old Indian trail in 1902. Fifteen miles farther along the divide, one reaches the Baker Pass trail, which is the last low point before heading north along the rugged peaks of the Never Summer Range. This pass was named for Jim Baker, a well-known mountain man who trapped beaver in this country in the 1820s and 1830s.

The eleven miles from Baker Pass to Thunder Pass contain several mountains that require careful planning. Carl Melzer's 1936 party skirted the entire Never Summer Range as a safety measure, but others have traversed some of the summits. The greatest difficulty is in carrying heavy overnight packs. Tom Melzer's group skirted

Lead, Tepee, and Richthofen peaks on the west side and portions of Cumulus, although they did reach the top of that "cloud" peak. They also skirted Static Peak, but climbed both Lulu and Thunder mountains. Tom's party camped near Mount Cirrus and made a separate climb of it while leaving their packs at camp. The route taken by the Melzers in 1976 as they skirted Mount Richthofen and Static Peak took them north of the divide to Lake Agnes, then along the Upper Michigan Ditch to the Michigan River, and then back to the divide at Lulu Mountain.

Thunder Pass is also known as Lulu Pass and was used by miners living in the old town of Lulu City, now a ghost town within Rocky Mountain National Park, to travel to the North Park area. Lulu City was named for the daughter of its founder, Benjamin Burnett. Once Mount Neota is crossed, the divide drops down to the service road at La Poudre Pass.

La Poudre Pass   Mile 139.5

La Poudre Pass takes its name from French trappers working for the American Fur Company, who made a cache of powder kegs to lighten their loads near La Porte, Colorado. The name Cache la Poudre was given to the river after the incident. During the 1870s and 1880s, La Poudre Pass was used for stagecoach service to the mining town of Lulu City. It now serves as an access road to the Longdraw Reservoir and Grandview Campground. The road goes within a quarter-mile of the divide and makes a good supply point.

From La Poudre Pass to Milner Pass on Trail Ridge Road, only Specimen Mountain's 12,489-foot summit must be crossed. The top offers wonderful views of the upcoming expanse of Rocky Mountain National Park as well as that of the rugged Never Summers to the west.

Milner Pass   Mile 145

Milner Pass marks the beginning of the major portion of Rocky Mountain National Park and the unique problems which exist there for one planning a divide hike. The pass was named for T. J. Milner, an early Colorado railroad engineer, and carries U.S. 34 across the divide at an elevation of 10,758 feet. The pass is by no means the high point of Trail Ridge Road, however, as Trail Ridge peaks at 12,183 feet, making it the highest road with a U.S. highway designation.

Anyone planning a divide hike through Rocky Mountain National Park must be aware of the current rules and regulations the National Park Service enforces for backpacking and camping within the park. Reservations must be made well in advance for camping spots and backcountry permits are required for specific sites and dates. It is illegal to camp on the tundra along the divide ridge and one must drop down to either the established campsites or one of the "cross-country zones" which allow more freedom to the low impact style of camper. Write to Rocky Mountain National Park, Estes Park, Colorado 80517-8397 for current information.

Most of the twenty-six miles from Milner Pass to the southern park boundary present no great difficulty. Glaciation on the eastern side of the ridge is very apparent and impressive while relatively gentle slopes on the west side offer easy hiking. Hallett Peak, for example, is well known from viewpoints above Bear, Dream, and Nymph lakes and is one of the most photographed mountains in the park. Its western side, however, is very gentle and can easily be climbed with overnight packs. The mountain was named for William L. Hallett, one of Colorado's earliest mountain climbers, who moved to Estes Park from New England in the 1870s.

The most difficult portion of the divide in the park is encountered at McHenrys Peak. The jagged notch on the north side of McHenrys is a stopping point and all those with whom I have talked have dropped off the divide near Powell Peak into the "cross-country zone" camping area of North Inlet Valley. The 1976 Melzer party saw large herds of elk and many beautiful waterfalls in this area. Continuing back to the divide, one can go by way of Lake Powell (the little one) and Chief's Head Peak, the summit of which is not actually on the divide ridge. Longs Peak is directly east of this area and fine views of its western side appear.

To avoid more difficult areas along the ridges of Mount Alice, The Cleaver, and Isolation Peak, it may be more practical to stay in lower country all the way from North Inlet to East Inlet and Paradise Creek, picking up the divide again on the southern slope

Pointed Navajo Peak, 13,409 feet, rises above Lake Isabel in the Indian Peaks Wilderness Area. These jagged ridges mark the center of the most formidable section of the divide in Colorado. Ron Ruhoff

of Isolation Peak. Doug Stewart climbed Mount Alice, but found the north ridge to be rather rough.

Ouzel Peak offers an easy summit and the last stretch to Ogalalla Peak at the southern park boundary is easily accomplished. From there, four and one-half miles of relatively easy ridges lead past the St. Vrain Glaciers and to Buchanan Pass.

Buchanan Pass marks the beginning of the longest "impassable" section of Colorado's divide. The many jagged summits of the Arapaho Range within the Indian Peaks Wilderness Area coincide with a continental divide ridge that is far too difficult to attempt for most hikers. One problem is that even if one is technically able to traverse the ridges, the time involved is probably prohibitive. Those who have completed Colorado's divide have dropped off the ridge to the west at Buchanan Pass, hiking the pass trail down to Monarch Lake, then following the Arapaho Pass trail back to the divide before continuing south.

From Arapaho Pass, the next 100 miles of the divide ridge, are familiar territory for me, as this is the portion which I describe in detail in my own adventure. The first difficulty encountered south of Arapaho Pass is the north ridge of Mount Neva. Although the summit is easily climbed, portions of the north ridge should be avoided. The rest of the way to Rollins Pass is easily traversed, again through country which is heavily glaciated on the east side and gentle sloping to the west. Devils Thumb Pass offers an interesting close-up view of the tall rock from which the name is derived.

Rollins Pass   *Mile 195*

Rollins Pass, often incorrectly called Corona Pass, was a standard gauge railroad crossing of the continental divide prior to the construction of the Moffat Tunnel. The Denver and Salt Lake Railroad, known as "The Moffat Road" after founder David Moffat, operated over the 11,671-foot pass for over eighteen years before the rails finally went "through" the divide when the Moffat Tunnel was completed in 1927. During its years of operation, the station atop the pass, called "Corona," was completely covered by snow sheds, and winter operations often required superhuman effort to keep the rails open.

The pass can be reached in passenger cars from Winter Park on the west. On the top, scattered boards indicate the location of the old Corona station. The east side of the pass is passable only in 4WD vehicles, because of a rough detour around the two original railroad trestles that have been closed to traffic since the late 1970s. A cave-in at the Needles Eye Tunnel was finally cleared and reopened for automobile traffic in the fall of 1987, and it is hoped that restoration work may someday reopen the trestles.

From Rollins Pass, the divide crosses one of the most often viewed group of mountains in Colorado. From Genesee Park on I-70, one can see the entire section of the divide from Rollins Pass south to Berthoud Pass, including the peaks of James, Bancroft, Parry, Eva, Flora, and Colorado Mines. The entire section offers easy hiking and, if one needs a campsite along the way, I suggest the little grassy shelf above Ice Lake.

Berthoud Pass   Mile 209.5

Berthoud Pass is the next year-round paved highway crossing of the divide and is the location of one of Colorado's earliest ski areas. A restaurant is located atop the pass, which was explored by Edward L. Berthoud in 1861. The divide is an easy hike along its crest from Berthoud Pass, over Stanley and Vasquez peaks, to Jones Pass at mile 219. Along the way, the old Vasquez Pass trail crosses. Vasquez Pass took its name from mountain man Louis Vasquez, whose name was also placed on the Vasquez Fork of the Platte River before it became known as Clear Creek. Jones Pass offers drivable access to the divide from the east by 4WD, but deadends at the old Bobtail Mine and Denver Water Board maintenance buildings on the west.

South of Jones Pass, the 13,553-foot summit of Pettingel Peak is encountered. Pettingel is not difficult, but the north ridge of the Citadel has a vertical cliff, recognizable by a streak of black rock, that will stop many people. Having climbed to both sides of this cliff with my overnight pack, I now know that I could climb it in the north to south direction. If you don't mind some rock climbing and have some rope along to lift packs up, you will be able to attain the summit of the Citadel without great difficulty. To avoid this one bad spot, you may prefer to drop into Bobtail Creek from Pettingel and skirt the Citadel entirely. Hagar Peak offers the last jumble of sharp rocks prior to Loveland Pass. Along the way, you will be directly above the Eisenhower Tunnel and can easily see I-70 emerging from the two portals.

Loveland Pass   Mile 231

U.S. 6 across Loveland Pass is still kept open year-round despite the Eisenhower Tunnel. The pass offers an alternate route for hazardous loads and a direct drive to the popular ski areas at Arapaho Basin and Keystone. Southeast of the pass, the divide crosses 13,427-foot Grizzly Peak and then crosses the only two peaks that surpass 14,000 feet on the continental divide in the United States, Grays and Torreys peaks. Both are easy climbs and many people will be encountered on these popular summits. The mountains

Mountain goats also enjoy climbing along the divide, frequently with much less effort! Mother and kid were photographed on the very summit of Grays Peak. Linda K. Peterson

Climbers atop Grays Peak try to escape from the wind in the remains of an old turn-of-the-century weather station. Ron Ruhoff

Torreys Peak, 14,267 feet, and Grays Peak, 14,270 feet, tower above the ghost town of Saints John. These are the only two fourteeners on the divide in Colorado and Grays Peak marks the highest point on the divide in North America except for the volcanoes of Mexico. Ron Ruhoff

were named for two early American botanists, Asa Gray and John Torrey.

The summit of 13,850-foot Mount Edwards must be crossed before dropping down to 13,207-foot Argentine Pass, accessible only from the east side in 4WD vehicles. The pass is completely rockslid on its west side, but was a popular route between Georgetown and Peru Creek in earlier days when it was also known as Sanderson or Snake River Pass. Argentine Pass has the distinction of being the highest drivable continental divide pass in North America. The Argentine Pass to Georgia Pass section offers no particular obstacle and is covered more completely in my personal account.

Georgia Pass   Mile 259

Georgia Pass is drivable in most automobiles from Jefferson and can be used as a fairly reliable supply point. The west side down to Breckenridge is strictly 4WD. The name derived from Georgia Gulch in the mining area on the west side where prospectors from the gold mining country of Georgia settled. Mount Guyot and Bald Mountain are crossed before the next vehicle access at Boreas Pass.

Boreas Pass   Mile 266

Boreas Pass, the old route of the Denver, South Park & Pacific Railroad, is an excellent dirt car road and offers a good route to the divide from either Breckenridge or Como. An easy seven-mile hike across Red Mountain takes one to the next highway at Hoosier Pass.

Hoosier Pass   Mile 273.5

Named by people from Indiana, Hoosier Pass is the route of Colorado 9 between Fairplay and Breckenridge. From here to Fremont Pass, the divide includes North Star Mountain, where many old miners' shacks are found near its crest, Wheeler Peak, where caution is advised and some skirting of jagged ridges will probably be necessary, and finally, the Climax Molybdenum Mine at Fremont Pass. Although the large open pit mine has ceased operations at this writing, it is necessary to cross AMAX property when following the divide down the slopes of McNamee Peak to Fremont Pass. The property is guarded and you must ask permission of security personnel prior to this portion of the hike. Asking prior permission will also enable you to ascertain any hazardous operations, such as blasting, should mining activity resume.

Fremont Pass   Mile 282

Colorado 91 crosses this pass between Copper Mountain on I-70 and Leadville. The workings of the world's largest molybdenum mine occupy most of the area. Fremont Pass is one of the few drivable viewpoints for distant Mount of the Holy Cross. The next highway access is at Tennessee Pass, nine miles away, after passing Chalk Mountain and the Cooper Hill Ski Area.

Tennessee Pass   Mile 291

Tennessee Pass was named by miners from that state in the 1860s, but it was also used by John C. Fremont, while on his way to California in 1845. U.S. 24 connects Leadville with Minturn via this route. The Denver & Rio Grande Western Railroad also uses this pass and tunnels beneath the crest through a 2,500-foot bore.

The thirty-five miles between Tennessee and Independence passes is cut approximately in half by the Hagerman Pass road, a rough road passable only in 4WD vehicles. The pass is historically significant because the standard gauge rails of the Colorado Midland Railroad once crossed the divide at this point between Leadville and Aspen. Two different tunnels were used to penetrate the top of the pass, the original being the Hagerman Tunnel at 11,500 feet and later the Busk-Ivanhoe Tunnel at 10,700 feet. The lower tunnel was later known as the Carlton Tunnel and was used for automobile traffic in the 1920s and 1930s. Both are now abandoned and a third tunnel, the Boustead, carries water for the Frying Pan-Arkansas Diversion Project under the divide at this point. Hagerman Pass is also the route of the high-voltage transmission line from Glenwood Canyon to Denver, the same line that crosses Argentine Pass.

From Hagerman Pass south, the divide crosses Deer Mountain and Blue Peak, both in the 13,700-foot class. Nearby, within a mile and one-half of the divide, is Mount Massive, 14,421 feet, Colorado's second highest peak. The divide ridges are rough here, but passable with care. Some people have dropped down into the upper Frying Pan Creek drainage below Hagerman Pass and followed the trail south to meet the divide again at Deer Mountain.

Independence Pass   Mile 326.5

Independence Pass marks the mid-point between the Wyoming and New Mexico borders and carries Colorado 82 across the divide between Aspen and the Arkansas Valley. The pass was named for

The Three Apostles of the Sawatch Range are an awesome sight above a camp in Clear Creek Canyon near Winfield. North Apostle, Ice Mountain, and West Apostle are all hazardous climbs and are usually skirted by those hiking the divide ridge. Ron Kuhoff

the old mining town of Independence on the west side of the divide. William Belden discovered a rich vein of ore there on July 4, 1879. When the town got a post office, the name had to be changed to avoid a conflict with Independence, Missouri, and it was named Chipeta in honor of the wife of Ute Indian Chief Ouray. Then, during the relatively short life of the town, its name was changed several more times, first to Mammoth City, then Mount Hope, Farwell, Sparkill, and finally back to Independence. Several structures still remain and it is a ghost town worth visiting.

South of the pass, Grizzly Peak's jagged 13,988-foot summit offers a challenge that not all divide hikers have attempted. It has long, rough ridges and several parties have skirted it in the interest of safety in bad weather. Grizzly was once listed as a fourteener, but lost that status with updated surveys.

Another fifteen miles of high 13,000-foot peaks, many un-named, continue south to the next formidable section of the divide, The Three Apostles. North Apostle Peak, Ice Mountain, and West Apostle Peak are a beautiful sight from the Clear Creek area above the ghost town of Winfield, but all are difficult climbs. I know of no one who has fully traversed the divide along their ridges. Most parties skirt the entire area to the west and south by following the Timberline Trail. A variety of routes east out of the Texas Creek area again reach the divide.

The entire length of the divide from the Lake Pass Trail to Cottonwood Pass, a distance of some thirty miles, contains a considerable number of unnamed 12,000 and 13,000-foot peaks. One of the most impressive summits, when viewed from the Buena Vista area, is 12,730-foot Birthday Peak, located at the head of Texas Creek. It offers an easy climb, however, as one continues south along the ridge. Beyond Birthday Peak is the Browns Pass trail and Cottonwood Pass.

Cottonwood Pass   *Mile 371*

Cottonwood Pass is an automobile road, open during summer and fall, which connects Buena Vista with the Taylor Park area. Its 12,126-foot summit offers magnificent views of the distant Elk Range to the west. The jagged ridges of Castle and Cathedral peaks are particularly evident. From Cottonwood Pass, ten miles of divide lead over several unnamed peaks as well as two thirteeners, Kreutzer and Emma Burr, before reaching the 4WD road at Tincup Pass.

Tincup Pass is a favorite 4WD route from St. Elmo to the old mining town of Tincup in Taylor Park and has been used by some divide hikers as a supply point. Historically, the pass was named after the town, which took its name from the fact that early prospector Fred Lottis panned for gold in the area with a tin cup.

Continuing south over Fitzpatrick Peak, one eventually comes to Altman Pass where the old Alpine Tunnel passes beneath the divide. The Denver, South Park & Pacific Railroad once ran through this country on its way from the Arkansas Valley to Pitkin and Gunnison. The tunnel was closed in 1910 after twenty-nine years of operation. The interior was lined with redwood timbers to strengthen the walls of rock and these are still intact today. I had the pleasure of walking inside the tunnel in 1966 when it was possible to gain access through a small crawl space at the west portal. The east end is entirely caved in and completely flooded.

Ron Ruhoff pauses at the Alpine Tunnel Railroad Station while on an overnight snowshoe trip across Altman Pass. The handiwork of Francis Trudgeon is evident in the signs, windows, and new roofing. Rex Myers

Portions of the tunnel that were not shored up with redwood have caved in over the many years since the last train passed through. The tunnel is extremely dangerous and should be avoided.

It is possible to drive a car to the west portal and visit the old depot which is still standing. Part of the stone engine house also still remains. For many years, Francis Trudgeon dedicated his time to the restoration and upkeep of the Alpine Tunnel Station and even today, although over eighty, he continues to work with members of the Mile-Hi Jeep Club in keeping this historic building in good condition.

It happens that three of the mountain peaks on the divide ridge near the Alpine Tunnel are named for old friends of mine who have since passed away. Mount Helmers is the 12,858-foot high point north of Altman Pass and it honors Dow Helmers who wrote *Historic Alpine Tunnel*. Mount Poor, the 12,442-foot high point south of the pass, is named for Mac Poor, author of *Denver, South Park & Pacific*, published by the Rocky Mountain Railroad Club in 1949. I shared many fine railroad excursions with both Mac and Dow over the years and think it wonderful that their names have been

The dedication of a new marker at the west portal of the Alpine Tunnel on August 27, 1967 resulted in this historic photograph. Standing left to right, are Dow Helmers, author of Historic Alpine Tunnel, Donald F. Smith, author of Chalk Creek to the Past, and Herbert D. Renck, the last surviving worker on the Denver, South Park & Pacific Railroad's Alpine Tunnel branch. Seated are Mac C. Poor (left), author of Denver, South Park and Pacific, and Francis Trudgeon, who has dedicated much of his life since 1958 to restoration projects at the west portal. Ron Ruhoff

placed on two continental divide summits.

Louisa Ward Arps, Colorado author and longtime member of the Colorado Mountain Club, also has a mountain named in her honor. The first peak immediately south of the old Williams Pass road is 12,383 feet high and named Mount Arps. I had the pleasure of knowing Louisa for many years as a fellow member of the Ghost Town Club of Colorado.

Williams Pass is a drivable 4WD road, but it has some extremely rough and boggy sections. Hancock Pass at mile 392 is the most often traveled road over the divide in this vicinity, offering an easy crossing from Chalk Creek over to the Alpine Tunnel and Pitkin. Eleven miles of divide connect Hancock Pass with U.S. 50 at Monarch Pass. Just prior to Monarch, Old Monarch Pass is crossed. This road is drivable by car during the summer months and was the crossing of the divide prior to the construction of the new highway. There is an even older route across the divide here, sometimes called Old Old Monarch, that coincides with some of the access roads on the slopes of the Monarch Ski Area.

Monarch Pass   Mile 403

Monarch Pass took its name from the early mining town of Monarch on its east side, where the present-day limestone quarry is located. From Monarch's crest, where a large parking area is located, one can hike up the divide ridge next to the gondola ride. At the crest, where visitors view distant scenery from the top of the gondola, you will be situated among many radio towers at an elevation of 11,898 feet. Continuing on to Marshall Pass, eleven miles south, a crossing is made of Chipeta Mountain, named for the wife of Ute Indian Chief Ouray.

Marshall Pass   Mile 414

Marshall Pass was once the crossing of the Denver & Rio Grande Railway's narrow gauge line to Gunnison, Montrose, and Ouray. It is a fine dirt road which leaves U.S. 285 at Mears Junction, north of Poncha Pass, and comes out on the west on U.S. 50 at Sargents. Marshall Pass marks the beginning of a fifty five-mile section of the divide which has some unique problems. The Cochetopa Hills are, for the most part, below timberline and contain a vast number of trails and dirt roads that criss cross the divide in all directions. It is very easy to lose the actual divide ridge in this area and careful study with maps and compass is necessary. Water is also a serious concern. Those who have traversed this area report that many streams shown on the maps will prove to be dry. What little water there is will almost certainly be contaminated from the grazing of sheep and cattle. Carrying a sufficient quantity of water is a must.

The newly completed Colorado Trail traverses the Cochetopa Hills area, often close to the divide. A guide of this route from Denver to Durango became available in 1988 and the trail will no doubt be helpful as a more reliable route through this problem area.

North Pass   Mile 444.5

Colorado 114 at North Pass marks the midpoint of the Cochetopa Hills and is a suggested supply point for at least water. This highway crossing replaced the older Cochetopa Pass crossing of Colorado 114 a few years ago. The word "cochetopa" means "pass of the buffalo" in the Ute language. This low country was no doubt a place where buffalo once grazed and crossed freely from one side of the divide to the other. Cochetopa Pass itself, at mile 449, remains a usable auto road.

Fourteen miles beyond North Pass, a 4WD road leaves the main road at Salt House Pass and goes west through the southwest corner of section 12. Along this road, there are two developed natural springs where cold running water is available. Salt House Pass was named for the structure on top where salt blocks for stock are stored. The road across the pass, Forest Service 787, is a good access to the divide except perhaps in rainy weather. The pass was once a stagecoach route and the springs have been used since early times.

Table Mountain marks the end of the Cochetopa Hills and the entrance into the La Garita Mountains. Although fifty-seven miles of hiking are required to get from North Pass to the next major crossing at Spring Creek Pass, some have used the roads into the Salt House Pass area as an access point. These roads are reliably passable most of the time and a Forest Service campground is located at the Stone Cellar Forest Service Station.

Several unnamed mountains in the 12,000 and 13,000-foot class are crossed prior to Spring Creek Pass. The La Garita Mountains take their name from the Spanish word for "the lookout," apparently from the fact that Ute Indians signaled one another from these summits to areas on the eastern side of the San Luis Valley. Just prior to the San Luis Pass trail, 14,014-foot San Luis Peak rises about two miles north of the divide. San Luis Pass can be approached very closely in a 4WD vehicle from the Willow Creek road north of Creede, making it a possible access point. The La Garita Wilderness Area is traversed from mile 474 south of Table Mountain to Mile 489 west of San Luis Pass. The 13,383-foot summit of Baldy Cinco is the last high point prior to the Colorado 149 crossing at

Spring Creek Pass. Colorado 149 is now paved all of the way from Creede to Lake City.

Spring Creek Pass   *Mile 501.5*

At Spring Creek Pass, the longest section of the Colorado divide between two automobile access points begins. It is 110 miles from Spring Creek Pass to Wolf Creek Pass, but what spectacular miles they are! The divide makes a large loop westward and then back again as it circles the headwaters of the Rio Grande through the great San Juan Mountains. One of the most prominent peaks of the San Juans, 13,821-foot Rio Grande Pyramid, is plainly visible for most of this section and will be climbed at mile 555.

If necessary, two 4WD passes can be counted on for access to the divide between Spring Creek and Wolf Creek passes. Carson Pass, at the ghost town of Carson, is a good 4WD road above Lake City along Wager Gulch. It is, however, no longer possible to drive the Lost Trail Creek route from Carson to Rio Grande Reservoir as people have done in years past.

The Stony Pass 4WD road is a popular route between Creede and Silverton and offers access from either side, the Silverton side being the shortest and in better condition. If you drive up the east side of Stony Pass from Lost Trail Campground, a left turn up Bear Creek (4WD) leads to the ghost town of Beartown and the Sylvanite mine at Kite Lake, directly beneath the continental divide ridge. The Hunchback Pass trail is easily reached from this point and leads directly into the Weminuche Wilderness Area. The divide ridge will be within the boundaries of this large and wonderfully scenic wilderness all the way to Lobo Overlook above Wolf Creek Pass. The Weminuche is Colorado's largest wilderness, containing 405,000 acres.

The great notch known as "the Window" is encountered one mile before Rio Grande Pyramid and is a spot that must be skirted. The pyramid itself is not too difficult a climb, if time and weather permit. The summit offers one of the most outstanding views of any peak in Colorado.

Rio Grande Pyramid marks the mid-point between Spring

Rio Grande Pyramid, 13,821 feet, and "the Window" are prominent landmarks on the San Juan loop of the divide. Douglas Barr

Creek and Wolf Creek passes. The second section offers no great difficulty, although Wes Mauz cautions that the area between mile 580 and 587 is quite dry. Be prepared to carry sufficient water south of Williams Lake. Natural springs are available at the western boundary of section 34, where it intersects the divide west of Palomino Mountain.

There are some delightful hot springs on the map in section 23 four miles south of South River Peak. You may want to follow the trail from a mile west of South River Peak down the West Fork of the San Juan River to enjoy the springs as Doug Barr and Dave Miller did. The divide can be accessed again by way of the Beaver Creek Trail to Sawtooth Mountain or you may want to shortcut over to U.S. 160.

Just prior to Wolf Creek Pass, the dirt car road to Lobo Overlook is reached. This road serves as access to the AT&T microwave tower there and offers a parking lot and view of Wolf Creek Pass and the beautiful San Juan valley.

Wolf Creek Pass   Mile 611.5

From Wolf Creek Pass south, much of the divide ridge is followed closely by the Continental Divide trail. Numerous other trails also criss-cross this area and it is easy to get off on the wrong one. Treasure Pass is crossed at mile 612.8 The trail crossing was named for nearby Treasure Mountain, so-called because of a legendary treasure of gold buried there. Treasure Falls, located near U.S. 160, is a delight to view with its lacy 100-foot drop.

Elwood Pass at mile 626.2 is a drivable auto road from the east side if the weather is dry. The roads around Summitville and Elwood Pass north of Platoro can be treacherously muddy in rainy weather. The west side is strictly 4WD.

Summit Peak's 13,300-foot summit is reported to be a large, rough mountain which the 1976 Melzer party skirted. From there to the New Mexico border, no technical difficulties are encountered. Blue Lake is very close to the divide ridge at mile 646 and might be a choice campsite because the next sixteen miles to Banded Lake lack usable water. Five more miles of hiking brings you to the last high point of Colorado's divide on Chama Peak's 12,021-foot summit. From here, the last eight miles are all downhill to the New Mexico line

New Mexico Border   Mile 673

The continental divide ridge is very indistinct as it crosses the state line. Private land covers portions of this area and should be avoided. The true divide crosses the state line about a mile and a half west of a county road where most people end their journey.

The preceding description of the Colorado continental divide is not meant to be complete to the last detail. Many variations will always be necessary depending on weather, technical climbing experience, transportation arrangements, and supply points. It is hoped that this overview will be helpful in making your own plans. ▲

Mark Bonomo takes in the beauty of it all on the divide near James Peak.
Ron Ruhoff

Appendix A

Points of Interest
On Colorado's Continental Divide

U.S. Geological Survey topographical maps are a must when planning a hike along the continental divide. I spent many hours studying these detailed maps to plan routes, distances, and access points. As a result, I felt that a complete list of all points of interest along the divide in Colorado would be an interesting and useful addition to this book. Even if one does not actually get out and hike along the divide, just following the ridge on topo maps can be a fascinating past-time.

In compiling the following list, the mileages were computed using a roller-type map measure, carefully rolling it along the divide ridge between peaks and passes. All mileages are rounded off to the nearest one-tenth-mile. Using this method, the total length of the divide from Wyoming to New Mexico is 672.7 miles. When a casual measurement is made with the same roller system on a Colorado highway map, the total is only about 525 miles. The larger scale of the 7½ maps is necessary to make an accurate measurement of all of the intricate twistings and turnings of the divide. The actual walking distance will be greater than the total measured on a flat map because of the constant ups and downs of the ridge. The divide is a series of right triangles connected end to end, meaning you are walking the hypotenuses all the way.

A total of seventy-seven 7½-minute maps are required to cover the entire divide ridge in Colorado. When I started hiking the divide, many of the newer 7½-minute maps had not been completed and we used a number of the older 15-minute series. The more recently surveyed 7½-minute maps will almost always have different elevation figures as newer surveying methods constantly update the accuracy of elevations. The U.S.G.S. maps are available at the self-serve map sales office in the Federal Building at 1961 Stout Street in downtown Denver, from the map sales office at the Federal Center at West Alameda Avenue and Kipling Street in Lakewood, and from many outdoor stores.

A more general coverage of the divide in Colorado can be gotten with only five U.S. Forest Service maps. From north to south they are, Routt, Roosevelt, Arapaho, San Isabel, and Rio Grande national forests. I highly recommend the purchase of these maps in addition to the topo series because of their better coverage of campgrounds, highways and other access roads, U.S. Forest Service boundaries, and other helpful details. The Forest Service maps are available at the headquarters building at 8th Avenue and Quail Street in Lakewood or from many outdoor stores.

All major highway crossings are listed in the chart with the official elevation from the latest Colorado Department of Highways map. All drivable passes, whether automobile or four-wheel-drive, appear in **bold** type. The names of mountain ranges, wilderness areas, and Rocky Mountain National Park are listed in the chart to indicate the location of their boundaries. Names followed by an asterisk (*) designate summits of peaks not on the divide ridge; nevertheless, the elevation of the summit is shown.

Name	Elevation	Mile Prev	7½' Quad Map	USFS Map	Total
Wyoming border	9,360	0.0	Dudley Creek, WY	Routt	0.0
USFS Road 412	9,260	0.5	West Fork Lake	Routt	0.5
Ellis Trail (jeep road)	9,450	5.3	West Fork Lake	Routt	5.8
Buck Mountain	11,372	11.1	Davis Peak	Routt	16.9
Main Fork Trail	9,840	2.9	Mount Zirkel	Routt	19.8
Fryingpan Trail	11,680	5.3	Mount Zirkel	Routt	25.1
Mount Zirkel	12,180	2.0	Mount Zirkel	Routt	27.1
Red Dirt Pass (trail)	11,530	1.3	Mount Zirkel	Routt	28.4
Flattop Mountain	12,118	1.7	Mount Zirkel	Routt	30.1
Ute Pass (trail)	11,000	1.2	Mount Zirkel	Routt	31.3
Wyoming Trail	10,900	2.6	Mount Zirkel	Routt	33.9
Lost Ranger Peak	11,932	6.6	Mount Ethel	Routt	40.5
Mount Ethel	11,924	4.4	Mount Ethel	Routt	44.9
Buffalo Pass (USFS Road 60)	10,300	9.2	Buffalo Pass	Routt	54.1
Percy Lake Trail	10,090	6.6	Mount Werner	Routt	60.7
Rabbit Ears Pass (US 40)	9,426	8.6	Rabbit Ears Peak	Routt	69.3

Left margin labels: SIERRA MADRE R. / MOUNT ZIRKEL WILDERNESS / PARK RANGE

Name	Elevation	Mile Prev	7 ½' Quad Map	USFS Map	Total
Baker Mountain	9,824	2.3	Rabbit Ears Peak	Routt	71.6
Muddy Pass (US 40)	8,772	1.7	Rabbit Ears Peak	Routt	73.3
Bear Mountain	9,845	3.2	Lake Agnes	Routt	76.5
Diamond Mountain*	9,442	2.7	Rabbit Ears Peak	Routt	79.2
Arapaho Pass (primitive road)	9,050	3.5	Spicer Peak	Routt	82.7
North Rider Peak	9,844	1.6	Whiteley Peak	Routt	84.3

(Many dirt roads criss-cross and follow divide along entire Rabbit Ears Range)

Name	Elevation	Mile Prev	7 ½' Quad Map	USFS Map	Total
Sheep Mountain	11,819	15.9	Hyannis Peak	Routt	100.2
Arapaho Creek Trail	11,220	0.6	Hyannis Peak	Routt	100.8
Troublesome Pass (primitive road)	10,027	4.1	Parkview Mountain	Routt	104.9
Haystack Mountain	11,495	1.4	Parkview Mountain	Routt	106.3
Parkview Mountain (Fire Lkt.)	12,296	3.9	Parkview Mountain	Routt	110.2
Willow Creek Pass (CO Hwy 125)	9,621	3.3	Radial Mountain	Routt	113.5
Willow Pass Stock Trail	9,986	1.0	Radial Mountain	Routt	114.5
Radial Mountain	11,241	1.4	Radial Mountain	Routt	115.9
Illinois Pass (trail)	9,980	2.8	Radial Mountain	Routt	110.7
Ruby Mountain	12,008	4.4	Bowen Mountain	Routt	123.1
Bowen Pass (trail)	11,476	1.0	Bowen Mountain	Routt	124.1
Farview Mountain	12,246	1.5	Mount Richthofen	Routt	125.6
Parika Peak	12,394	0.5	Mount Richthofen	Routt	126.1
Baker Pass (trail)	11,253	2.4	Mount Richthofen	Routt	128.5
Mount Cumulus	12,725	1.3	Mount Richthofen	Routt	129.8
Howard Mountain	12,810	1.2	Mount Richthofen	Routt	131.0
Mount Cirrus	12,797	0.7	Mount Richthofen	Routt	131.7
Lead Mountain	12,537	1.0	Mount Richthofen	Routt	132.7
Tepee Mountain	12,370	1.1	Mount Richthofen	Routt	133.8
Mount Richthofen	12,940	0.6	Mount Richthofen	Routt	134.4
Static Peak	12,575	0.6	Mount Richthofen	Routt	135.0
Thunder or Lulu Pass (trail)	11,331	1.3	Fall River Pass	Routt	136.3
Lulu Mountain	12,228	0.6	Fall River Pass	Routt	136.9

RABBIT EARS RANGE

NEVER SUMMER RANGE

ROCKY MOUNTAIN N.P.

Name	Elevation	Mile Prev	7½' Quad Map	USFS Map	Total
Thunder Mountain	12,050	0.6	Fall River Pass	Routt	137.5
Mount Neota	11,734	0.6	Fall River Pass	Roosevelt	138.1
La Poudre Pass (service road)	10,175	1.4	Fall River Pass	Roosevelt	139.5
Grand Ditch Crossing	—	—	—	Roosevelt	—
Specimen Mountain	12,489	3.3	Fall River Pass	Roosevelt	142.8
Milner Pass (US 34)	10,758	2.1	Fall River Pass	Roosevelt	144.9
Mount Ida	12,880	4.0	Grand Lake	Roosevelt	148.9
Sprague Mountain	12,713	3.3	McHenrys Peak	Roosevelt	152.2
Sprague Pass (trail)	11,708	1.1	McHenrys Peak	Roosevelt	153.3
Knobtop Mountain	12,331	1.7	McHenrys Peak	Roosevelt	155.0
Ptarmigan Point	12,363	1.0	McHenrys Peak	Roosevelt	156.0
Ptarmigan Pass (trail)	12,190	0.2	McHenrys Peak	Roosevelt	156.2
Flattop Mountain	12,324	0.6	McHenrys Peak	Roosevelt	156.8
Hallett Peak	12,713	0.6	McHenrys Peak	Roosevelt	157.4
Otis Peak	12,486	1.1	McHenrys Peak	Roosevelt	158.5
Andrews Pass (Alva Adams Water Tun.)	11,980	0.5	McHenrys Peak	Roosevelt	159.0
Taylor Peak	13,153	1.1	McHenrys Peak	Roosevelt	160.1
Powell Peak	13,208	1.4	McHenrys Peak	Roosevelt	161.5
McHenrys Notch	12,820	0.2	McHenrys Peak	Roosevelt	161.7
McHenrys Peak	13,327	0.3	McHenrys Peak	Roosevelt	162.0
Stone Man Pass	12,490	0.4	McHenrys Peak	Roosevelt	162.4
Chiefs Head Peak*	13,579	0.9	Isolation Peak	Roosevelt	163.3
Mount Alice	13,310	1.6	Isolation Peak	Roosevelt	164.9
Boulder-Grand Pass	12,061	1.2	Isolation Peak	Roosevelt	166.1
Tanima Peak	12,420	0.5	Isolation Peak	Roosevelt	166.6
The Cleaver	12,250	0.6	Isolation Peak	Roosevelt	167.2
Isolation Peak	13,118	1.2	Isolation Peak	Roosevelt	168.4
Ouzel Peak	12,716	1.4	Isolation Peak	Roosevelt	169.8
Cony Pass	12,760	0.7	Isolation Peak	Roosevelt	170.5
Ogalalla Peak	13,138	0.6	Isolation Peak	Roosevelt	171.1
Buchanan Pass (trail)	11,837	4.5	Isolation Peak	Roosevelt	175.6
Sawtooth Mountain	12,260	0.4	Isolation Peak	Roosevelt	176.0
Paiute Peak	13,088	2.6	Monarch Lake	Roosevelt	178.6
Mount Toll	12,979	0.8	Monarch Lake	Roosevelt	179.4
Pawnee Peak	12,943	0.7	Monarch Lake	Roosevelt	180.1

N.S.R.

ROCKY MOUNTAIN NATIONAL PARK

A.R. (I.P.)

Name	Elevation	Mile Prev	7½' Quad Map	USFS Map	Total
Pawnee Pass (trail)	12,541	0.5	Monarch Lake	Roosevelt	180.6
Apache Peak	13,441	1.9	Monarch Lake	Roosevelt	182.5
Navajo Peak	13,409	0.5	Monarch Lake	Roosevelt	183.0
Arikaree Peak	13,150	0.8	Monarch Lake	Roosevelt	183.8
North Arapaho Peak	13,502	1.7	Monarch Lake	Roosevelt	185.5
South Arapaho Peak*	13,397	0.5	Monarch Lake	Roosevelt	186.0
Arapaho Pass (trail)	11,906	1.6	Monarch Lake	Roosevelt	187.6
Mount Neva	12,814	1.2	Monarch Lake	Roosevelt	188.8
Jasper Peak	12,923	1.3	East Portal	Roosevelt	190.1
Devil's Thumb Pass (trail)	11,747	1.6	East Portal	Roosevelt	191.7
Rollins Pass (dirt road)	11,671	3.4	East Portal	Roosevelt	195.1
CAA Radio Beacon (abandoned)	12,072	1.8	East Portal	Roosevelt	196.9
Moffat R.R. Tunnel	—	1.8	East Portal	Roosevelt	198.7
Rogers Pass (4WD road)	11,860	2.0	Empire	Roosevelt	200.7
Ute Trail	12,300	0.9	Empire	Roosevelt	201.6
James Peak	13,294	0.6	Empire	Roosevelt	202.2
Mount Bancroft	13,200	1.2	Empire	Arapaho	203.4
Parry Peak	13,391	0.7	Empire	Arapaho	204.1
Mount Eva	13,130	0.9	Empire	Arapaho	205.0
Mount Flora	13,132	2.0	Empire	Arapaho	207.0
Colorado Mines Peak	12,493	1.8	Berthoud Pass	Arapaho	208.8
Berthoud Pass (US 40)	11,315	0.8	Berthoud Pass	Arapaho	209.6
Stanley Mountain	12,521	3.3	Berthoud Pass	Arapaho	212.9
Vasquez Pass (trail)	11,690	0.4	Berthoud Pass	Arapaho	213.3
Vasquez Peak	12,947	1.9	Berthoud Pass	Arapaho	215.2
VABM Bobtail	12,803	3.0	Byers Peak	Arapaho	218.2
Jones Pass (dirt road)	12,451	0.6	Byers Peak	Arapaho	218.8
Pettingell Peak	13,553	4.2	Loveland Pass	Arapaho	223.0
The Citadel	13,294	1.1	Loveland Pass	Arapaho	224.1
Hagar Mountain	13,195	0.7	Loveland Pass	Arapaho	224.8
Eisenhower Tunnel (I-70)	—	2.3	Loveland Pass	Arapaho	227.1
Loveland Pass (US 6)	11,992	4.0	Loveland Pass	Arapaho	231.1
un-named	13,117	1.7	Grays Peak	Arapaho	232.8
Irwin Pass (old trail)	12,756	0.3	Grays Peak	Arapaho	233.1

Side labels: **A.R. (I.P.)**, **FRONT RANGE**

Name	Elevation	Mile Prev	7½' Quad Map	USFS Map	Total
Grizzly Peak	13,427	0.8	Grays Peak	Arapaho	233.9
Torreys Peak	14,267	1.7	Grays Peak	Arapaho	235.6
Grays Peak	14,270	0.7	Grays Peak	Arapaho	236.3
Mount Edwards	13,850	1.3	Grays Peak	Arapaho	237.6
Argentine Pass (4WD road)	13,207	1.1	Grays Peak	Arapaho	238.7
Argentine Peak	13,738	1.0	Montezuma	Arapaho	239.7
Shoshone Plant highline	13,525	0.3	Montezuma	Arapaho	240.0
Decatur Mountain	12,890	1.4	Montezuma	Arapaho	241.4
Revenue Mountain	12,889	1.1	Montezuma	Arapaho	242.5
Silver Mountain	12,849	0.7	Montezuma	Arapaho	243.2
Santa Fe Peak	13,180	1.6	Montezuma	Arapaho	244.8
Sullivan Mountain	13,134	0.7	Montezuma	Arapaho	245.5
Roberts water tunnel	—	0.1	Montezuma	Arapaho	245.6
Geneva Peak	13,266	0.7	Montezuma	Arapaho	245.3
Landslide Peak	13,238	0.4	Montezuma	Arapaho	245.7
un-named	13,214	1.0	Montezuma	Arapaho	247.7
Webster Pass (4WD road)	12,096	1.2	Montezuma	Arapaho	248.9
Handcart Peak	12,518	0.9	Montezuma	Arapaho	249.8
Handcart Pass (old trail)	12,250	0.5	Montezuma	Arapaho	250.3
USLM Bullion	12,948	2.9	Montezuma	Arapaho	253.2
Whale Peak	13,078	1.3	Jefferson	Arapaho	254.5
Glacier Peak	12,853	1.5	Boreas Pass	Arapaho	256.0
Georgia Pass (dirt road)	11,585	3.0	Boreas Pass	Arapaho	259.0
Mount Guyot	13,370	1.2	Boreas Pass	Arapaho	260.2
French Pass (trail)	12,046	1.8	Boreas Pass	Arapaho	262.0
Bald Mountain	13,679	1.0	Boreas Pass	Arapaho	263.0
Boreas Pass (dirt auto road)	11,481	2.9	Boreas Pass	Arapaho	265.9
Red Peak	13,213	2.7	Breckenridge	Arapaho	268.6
Hoosier Pass (CO Hwy 9)	11,541	4.9	Alma	Arapaho	273.5
North Star Mountain	13,614	2.8	Breckenridge	Arapaho	276.3
Wheeler Mountain* (Point C)	13,690	1.7	Copper Mountain	Arapaho	278.0

FRONT RANGE

M.R.

Name	Elevation	Mile Prev	7½' Quad Map	USFS Map	Total
Clinton Peak	13,857	1.2	Climax	San Isabel	279.2
McNamee Peak	13,770	0.5	Climax	San Isabel	279.7
Ceresco Ridge	—	—	Climax	San Isabel	—
Fremont Pass **(CO Hwy 91)**	11,318	2.1	Climax	San Isabel	281.8
Chalk Mountain	12,017	0.8	Climax	San Isabel	282.6
Cooper Hill	11,757	6.5	Leadville North	San Isabel	289.1
Tennessee Pass **(US 24)**	10,424	1.9	Leadville North	San Isabel	291.0
Wurt's Ditch & Road	10,620	2.4	Leadville North	San Isabel	293.4
Homestake Peak	13,209	2.9	Homestake Rsvr.	San Isabel	298.3
un-named	13,042	1.9	Homestake Rsvr.	San Isabel	300.2
Galena Mountain*	12,893	2.5	Homestake Rsvr.	San Isabel	302.7
Homestake Diversion Tunnel	—	1.1	Homestake Rsvr.	San Isabel	303.8
"Tyle"	12,189	4.2	Nast	San Isabel	308.0
"Divide"	12,259	2.4	Nast	San Isabel	310.4
Hagerman Pass **(dirt road)**	11,925	0.6	Homestake Rsvr.	San Isabel	311.0
Rousted Diversion Tunnel	—	0.2	Homestake Rsvr.	San Isabel	311.2
Busk-Ivanhoe Tunnel	—	0.5	Homestake Rsvr.	San Isabel	311.7
Hagerman railroad tunnel	—	0.2	Homestake Rsvr.	San Isabel	311.9
Busk-Ivanhoe Peak	12,334	0.3	Mount Massive	San Isabel	312.2
Deer Mountain	13,761	7.8	Mount Champion	San Isabel	320.0
Blue Peak	13,711	4.4	Mount Champion	San Isabel	324.4
Independence Pass **(CO Hwy 82)**	12,093	2.2	Independence Pass	San Isabel	326.6
Grizzly Peak	13,988	6.4	Independence Pass	San Isabel	333.0
Garfield Peak	13,660	1.0	Independence Pass	San Isabel	335.0
Red Mountain	13,450	0.5	Independence Pass	San Isabel	335.5
un-named	13,312	2.7	Pieplant	San Isabel	337.2
Lake Pass (trail)	12,250	2.0	Pieplant	San Isabel	339.2
un-named	13,322	0.5	Pieplant	San Isabel	339.7
un-named	13,295	2.0	Pieplant	San Isabel	341.7
un-named	13,015	1.0	Pieplant	San Isabel	342.7
un-named	13,050	0.7	Pieplant	San Isabel	343.4
un-named	13,235	2.4	Pieplant	San Isabel	345.8

M.R.

SAWATCH RANGE

Name	Elevation	Mile Prev	7½' Quad Map	USFS Map	Total
un-named	13,253	1.1	Winfield	San Isabel	346.9
un-named	13,175	2.0	Winfield	San Isabel	348.9
West Apostle Peak	13,568	1.0	Winfield	San Isabel	349.9
Ice Mountain	13,951	0.8	Winfield	San Isabel	350.7
North Apostle Peak	13,860	0.5	Winfield	San Isabel	351.2
un-named	13,517	1.1	Winfield	San Isabel	352.3
Emerald Peak*	13,904	3.5	Winfield	San Isabel	355.8
un-named	13,762	1.8	Mount Harvard	San Isabel	357.6
un-named	13,352	0.8	Mount Harvard	San Isabel	358.4
un-named	13,276	0.7	Mount Harvard	San Isabel	359.1
un-named	13,128	0.8	Mount Harvard	San Isabel	359.9
un-named	12,780	1.8	Mount Harvard	San Isabel	361.7
un-named	12,776	0.9	Mount Harvard	San Isabel	362.6
Birthday Peak	12,730	0.5	Mount Harvard	San Isabel	363.1
un-named	12,685	0.8	Mount Yale	San Isabel	363.9
un-named	12,778	0.8	Mount Yale	San Isabel	364.7
pack trail	12,490	0.3	Mount Yale	San Isabel	365.0
un-named	12,955	0.7	Mount Yale	San Isabel	365.7
Browns Pass (trail)	12,050	0.7	Mount Yale	San Isabel	366.4
un-named	12,524	0.8	Mount Yale	San Isabel	367.2
un-named	12,956	0.7	Mount Yale	San Isabel	367.9
Turner Peak*	13,233	1.4	Tincup	San Isabel	369.3
Cottonwood Pass (county road)	12,126	1.6	Tincup	San Isabel	370.9
un-named	12,792	1.7	Tincup	San Isabel	372.6
un-named	12,850	1.8	Tincup	San Isabel	374.4
un-named	13,055	0.6	Tincup	San Isabel	375.0
Mount Kreutzer	13,095	1.7	Tincup	San Isabel	376.7
Emma Burr Mountain	13,538	1.8	Cumberland Pass	San Isabel	378.5
Tincup Pass (4WD road)	12,154	2.3	Cumberland Pass	San Isabel	380.8
Fitzpatrick Peak	13,112	1.5	Cumberland Pass	San Isabel	382.3
un-named	12,885	1.8	Cumberland Pass	San Isabel	384.1
un-named	12,954	1.9	Cumberland Pass	San Isabel	386.0
Mount Helmers	12,858	0.9	Cumberland Pass	San Isabel	386.9
Altman Pass (Alpine Tunnel)	11,940	0.6	Cumberland Pass	San Isabel	387.5
Mount Poor	12,442	0.8	Cumberland Pass	San Isabel	388.3

SAWATCH RANGE

Name	Elevation	Mile Prev	7½' Quad Map	USFS Map	Total
Williams Pass (rough 4WD road)	11,766	0.7	Cumberland Pass	San Isabel	389.0
Mount Arps	12,383	0.7	Cumberland Pass	San Isabel	389.7
Mount Chapman	12,755	1.0	Cumberland Pass	San Isabel	390.7
Hancock Pass (4WD road)	12,125	0.9	Garfield	San Isabel	391.6
Van Wirt Mountain	13,024	1.3	Garfield	San Isabel	392.9
Monumental Peak	13,369	1.1	Garfield	San Isabel	394.0
Vulcan Mountain	12,973	1.3	Garfield	San Isabel	395.3
Clover Mountain	12,955	0.8	Garfield	San Isabel	396.1
Bald Mountain	12,856	1.3	Garfield	San Isabel	397.4
Old, Old Monarch Pass (Monarch Ski Area)	11,523	3.1	Garfield	San Isabel	400.5
Old Monarch Pass (dirt road)	11,375	1.4	Pahlone Peak	San Isabel	401.9
un-named	11,692	0.6	Pahlone Peak	San Isabel	402.5
Monarch Pass (US 50)	11,312	0.5	Pahlone Peak	San Isabel	403.0
Monarch Ridge gondola	11,090	0.1	Pahlone Peak	San Isabel	403.4
Mount Peck	12,208	1.9	Pahlone Peak	San Isabel	405.3
Peel Point	12,145	1.6	Pahlone Peak	San Isabel	406.9
un-named	12,195	1.2	Pahlone Peak	San Isabel	408.1
Chipeta Mountain	12,850	2.2	Mount Ouray	San Isabel	410.3
pack trail	12,290	0.9	Mount Ouray	San Isabel	411.2
un-named	12,685	0.8	Mount Ouray	San Isabel	412.0
Marshall Pass (county road)	10,840	2.1	Mount Ouray	San Isabel	414.1
Windy Peak	11,885	4.4	Chester	Rio Grande	418.5
natural gas pipeline	10,650	2.7	Chester	Rio Grande	421.2
Sargents Mesa (4WD roads)	11,719	7.8	Sargents Mesa	Rio Grande	429.0
Long Branch Baldy	11,974	6.3	Sargents Mesa	Rio Grande	435.3
Lujan-Spanish Creek (primitive road)	10,336	6.8	North Pass	Rio Grande	442.1
North Pass (CO Hwy 114)	10,149	2.4	North Pass	Rio Grande	444.5
Cochetopa Pass (county road)	10,032	4.5	North Pass	Rio Grande	449.0

SAWATCH RANGE

COCHETOPA HILLS

Name	Elevation	Mile Prev	7½' Quad Map	USFS Map	Total
Jakes Creek (4WD road)	10,225	2.0	North Pass	Rio Grande	451.0
Fourmile Creek Jeep Road	10,698	6.2	Saguache Park	Rio Grande	457.2
Salthouse Pass (USFS road)	10,650	1.7	Saguache Park	Rio Grande	458.9

(Many 4WD roads criss-cross the divide between Salthouse Pass and Table Mountain)

Name	Elevation	Mile Prev	7½' Quad Map	USFS Map	Total
un-named	11,504	2.3	Saguache Park	Rio Grande	461.2
Table Mountain	11,890	9.4	Elk Park	Rio Grande	470.6
Cochetopa Ditch	11,210	1.1	Halfmoon Pass	Rio Grande	471.7
un-named	13,402	5.0	Halfmoon Pass	Rio Grande	476.7
un-named	13,628	1.8	Halfmoon Pass	Rio Grande	478.5
un-named	13,495	0.8	San Luis Peak	Rio Grande	479.3
un-named	13,346	0.7	San Luis Peak	Rio Grande	480.0
un-named	12,798	1.4	San Luis Peak	Rio Grande	481.4
un-named	13,155	1.5	San Luis Peak	Rio Grande	482.9
un-named	12,935	1.0	San Luis Peak	Rio Grande	483.9
un-named	13,285	0.8	San Luis Peak	Rio Grande	484.7
Skyline Trail	12,330	1.7	San Luis Peak	Rio Grande	486.4
San Luis Pass (4WD near access)	12,050	1.0	San Luis Peak	Rio Grande	487.4
un-named	13,111	0.9	San Luis Peak	Rio Grande	488.3
4WD trail	12,850	0.4	San Luis Peak	Rio Grande	488.7
un-named	12,906	0.7	San Luis Peak	Rio Grande	489.4
un-named	13,034	1.5	Baldy Cinco	Rio Grande	490.9
un-named	12,952	1.5	Baldy Cinco	Rio Grande	492.4
Skyline Trail	12,550	3.1	Baldy Cinco	Rio Grande	495.5
Baldy Cinco	13,383	2.1	Baldy Cinco	Rio Grande	497.6
Spring Creek Pass (CO Hwy 149)	10,898	3.8	Slumgullion Pass	Rio Grande	501.4
"Buck" Jarosa Mesa	12,054	4.0	Slumgullion Pass	Rio Grande	505.4
un-named	12,305	2.7	Lake San Cristobal	Rio Grande	508.1
un-named	13,135	5.4	Lake San Cristobal	Rio Grande	513.5
Coney	13,334	2.0	Finger Mesa	Rio Grande	515.5
Carson Pass (4WD Road)	12,350	1.5	Finger Mesa	Rio Grande	517.0

Section labels (vertical, left margin): **COCHETOPA HILLS**, **LA GARITAS / LA GARITAS WILDERNESS**, **SAN JUAN MOUNTAINS**

Name	Elevation	Mile Prev	7½' Quad Map	USFS Map	Total
Bent Peak	13,393	1.0	Pole Creek Mount.	Rio Grande	518.0
Carson Peak	13,657	1.3	Pole Creek Mount.	Rio Grande	519.3
un-named	13,450	1.3	Pole Creek Mount.	Rio Grande	520.6
un-named	13,164	5.1	Pole Creek Mount.	Rio Grande	525.7
Canby Mountain	13,478	7.1	Howardsville	Rio Grande	532.8
Stony Pass (4WD road)	12,588	0.4	Howardsville	Rio Grande	533.2
un-named	13,165	0.5	Howardsville	Rio Grande	533.7
Hunchback Mountain	13,136	7.0	Storm King Peak	Rio Grande	540.7
Hunchback Pass (trail)	12,493	0.8	Storm King Peak	Rio Grande	541.5
un-named	13,110	1.4	Storm King Peak	Rio Grande	542.9
un-named	13,230	1.0	Rio Grande Pyramid	Rio Grande	543.9
un-named	13,169	1.4	Rio Grande Pyramid	Rio Grande	545.3
"Ute"	12,892	6.0	Rio Grande Pyramid	Rio Grande	551.3
"The Window"	12,857	2.7	Rio Grande Pyramid	Rio Grande	554.0
Rio Grande Pyramid	13,821	0.9	Rio Grande Pyramid	Rio Grande	554.9
un-named	13,278	1.2	Weminuche Pass	Rio Grande	556.1
Weminuche Pass (trail)	10,630	3.2	Weminuche Pass	Rio Grande	559.3
Raber Lohr Ditch	10,650	0.4	Weminuche Pass	Rio Grande	559.7
un-named	13,010	11.6	Cimarrona Peak	Rio Grande	561.3
"Hossick"	12,967	0.8	Cimarrona Peak	Rio Grande	572.1
Squaw Pass (trail)	11,200	1.4	Cimarrona Peak	Rio Grande	573.5
Palomino Mountain	12,230	16.8	Palomino Mountain	Rio Grande	590.3
Piedra Peak*	12,328	2.1	Palomino Mountain	Rio Grande	592.4
Piedra Pass (trail)	11,500	1.0	Palomino Mountain	Rio Grande	593.4
South River Peak*	13,148	1.2	South River Peak	Rio Grande	594.6
Sawtooth Mountain*	12,605	6.2	South River Peak	Rio Grande	600.8
Archuleta Lake*	11,750	1.7	South River Peak	Rio Grande	602.5
Lobo Overlook (dirt road)	11,750	8.2	Wolf Creek Pass	Rio Grande	610.7
Wolf Creek Pass (US 160)	10,850	0.7	Wolf Creek Pass	Rio Grande	611.4
Treasure Pass (trail)	11,742	1.4	Wolf Creek Pass	Rio Grande	612.8
Alberta Peak	11,870	1.0	Wolf Creek Pass	Rio Grande	613.8
un-named	11,590	1.3	Wolf Creek Pass	Rio Grande	615.1
Railroad Pass (trail)	11,750	1.5	Wolf Creek Pass	Rio Grande	616.6
Silver Pass (trail)	10,900	2.1	Elwood Pass	Rio Grande	618.7

SAN JUAN MOUNTAINS

WEMINUCHE WILDERNESS

Name	Elevation	Mile Prev	7½' Quad Map	USFS Map	Total
Bonito Pass (trail)	11,300	1.8	Elwood Pass	Rio Grande	620.5
Summit Pass (trail)	11,775	5.0	Elwood Pass	Rio Grande	625.5
Elwood Pass (4WD road)	11,631	0.7	Elwood Pass	Rio Grande	626.2
Montezuma Peak	13,150	4.4	Summit Peak	Rio Grande	630.6
Summit Peak	13,300	1.9	Summit Peak	Rio Grande	632.5
un-named	12,887	7.0	Summit Peak	Rio Grande	639.5
"Snow"	12,815	1.8	Summit Peak	Rio Grande	641.3
Gunsight Pass	—	0.3	Summit Peak	Rio Grande	641.6
un-named	12,727	0.2	Summit Peak	Rio Grande	641.8
Blue Lake*	11,463	4.1	Elephant Head Rock	Rio Grande	645.9
un-named	11,803	3.5	Victoria Lake & Archuleta Creek	Rio Grande	649.4
Banded Peak	12,778	10.5	Chama Peak	Rio Grande	659.9
un-named	11,383	1.6	Chama Peak	Rio Grande	661.5
un-named	11,855	2.4	Chama Peak	Rio Grande	663.9
Chama Peak	12,021	1.2	Chama Peak	Rio Grande	665.1
county road to Chama, NM	8,120	6.4	Chama Peak	Rio Grande	671.5
New Mexico border	9,054	1.2	Chromo Mtn., NM	Rio Grande	672.7

SAN JUAN MOUNTAINS

Mountain Range Abbreviations

Sierra Madre Range - **S.M.R.**
Park Range - **P.R.**
Rabbit Ears Range - **R.E.R.**
Never Summer Range - **N.S.R.**
Arapaho Range (Indian Peaks) - **A.R. (I.P.)**
Front Range - **F.R.**
Mosquito Range - **M.R.**
Sawatch Range - **S.R.**
Cochetopa Hills - **C.H.**
La Garitas - **L.G.**
San Juan Mountains - **S.J.M.**

▲

A Quick Reference
To Vehicle Access Points

The following is a quick reference to the major and most practical access points on Colorado's divide. Each pass listed is driveable in regular automobiles during the summer and fall. There are many additional accesses available to those using four-wheel-drive and are all listed in Appendix A. The mileages refer to the divide ridge distance between each access point.

Wyoming State Line
54.1 miles
Buffalo Pass Road (graded dirt road)
15.2 miles
Rabbit Ears Pass (US 40)
4.0 miles
Muddy Pass (US 40)
40.2 miles
Willow Creek Pass (CO Hwy 125)
26 miles
La Poudre Pass (graded dirt road)
5.4 miles
Milner Pass (US 34 / Trail Ridge Road)
50.2 miles
Rollins Pass (dirt road)
14.5 miles
Berthoud Pass (US 40)
21.5 miles
Loveland Pass (US 6)
27.9 miles
Georgia Pass (dirt road)
6.9 miles
Boreas Pass (graded dirt road)
7.6 miles

Hoosier Pass (CO Hwy 9)
8.3 miles
Fremont Pass (CO Hwy 91)
9.2 miles
Tennessee Pass (US 24)
35.6 miles
Independence Pass (CO Hwy 82)
44.3 miles
Cottonwood Pass (graded dirt road)
32.1 miles
Monarch Pass (US 50)
11.1 miles
Marshall Pass (graded dirt road)
30.4 miles
North Pass (CO Hwy 114)
56.9 miles
Spring Creek Pass (CO Hwy 149)
110 miles
Wolf Creek Pass (US 160)
61.3 miles
New Mexico State Line

▲

Appendix C

Suggested Shorter Hikes Along Colorado's Divide

While this book deals primarily with people who have hiked all or extensive portions of the Colorado divide, the divide ridge offers something for everyone, whether a day hike, an hour walk, or perhaps only a few minutes outside of one's car atop a pass. A visit to a divide pass can be an educational and enjoyable experience that clearly shows glaciation processes on the leeward side of the ridge. Children and adults alike, new to the mountain area, may find that standing on the actual place where water flows to one ocean or the other is something never to be forgotten.

There are endless possibilities for short hikes along the divide, including of course some of the shorter distances between highway passes. A few of my favorites, which do not involve shuttling cars, are the following.

Loveland Pass

One of the popular places to spend a little time on the divide ridge is atop Loveland Pass on U.S. 6. There is a short trail which follows the divide above the parking lot. One can walk up that hill and have fine views of both drainages, the Pacific side toward Arapaho Basin Ski Area and the Atlantic toward Loveland Basin. The jagged summit of the Citadel is plainly visible to the northwest. If you look at the ground along the way, many species of colorful alpine wildflowers are found and it is a good place to watch the activities of marmots, pikas, and perhaps some ptarmigan in their alpine tundra habitat. One hundred yards or so may be enough, or you may want to follow the ridge all the way to Grizzly Peak or even to Torreys Peak from this location.

Milner Pass - Trail Ridge Road

Of all the passes in Colorado that are drivable in an automobile, perhaps the Milner Pass crossing of the divide on Trail Ridge Road in Rocky Mountain National Park offers the best visual indications of the process of glaciation and the division of water between the two oceans. Trail Ridge Road offers many fine parking areas and viewpoints for people confined to their car for physical reasons.

Independence Pass

The popular summer drive over Independence Pass between Aspen and Leadville offers a chance for the casual walker to experience a bit of the divide ridge. From the parking area atop the pass, a short trail follows the divide south, ending on a slight rise with views of distant Grizzly Peak. To the west, the headwaters of the Roaring Fork River will eventually meet the Colorado River and flow to the Pacific. On the eastern slope, Lake Creek flows toward the Arkansas River and eventually the Mississippi River and the Gulf of Mexico.

Rollins Pass

One of the easiest sections of the high continental divide to hike that also offers spectacular views of abrupt glaciation and alpine lakes is located north of Rollins Pass. The dirt car road from Winter Park on the west offers easy access to the pass and the 3.4-mile hike north to Devil's Thumb Pass along the divide is very enjoyable. The views over precipitous cliffs to King, Betty, and Bob lakes are some of the most rewarding of all. This area of Colorado's divide ridge offers some of the most obvious evidence of the action of ancient glaciers.

▲

There are also several possibilities for one-day hikes between two highway passes. One such section from La Poudre Pass to Milner Pass in Rocky Mountain National Park is only 5.4-miles long. Other short sections offering automobile access at both ends include Rabbit Ears Pass to Muddy Pass, 4.0 miles; Georgia Pass to Boreas Pass, 6.9 miles; Boreas Pass to Hoosier Pass, 7.6 miles; Hoosier Pass to Fremont Pass, 8.3 miles; and Fremont Pass to Tennessee Pass, 9.2 miles.

Even on these shorter sections, one must always be aware of weather changes and make plans with your driver in case it becomes necessary to drop off the ridge to a different pickup point. Never attempt any section of the divide without appropriate maps and clothing in case of bad weather. Weather in Colorado has a way of changing very rapidly. ▲

Appendix D

Suggestions for Expedition Planning

Hiking the continental divide with overnight gear is not unlike any other backpacking, but it does involve some unique situations. These suggestions are not intended to be a complete guide for the beginning backpacker, as it is assumed that anyone planning a trek such as the divide will already be experienced in outdoor travel.

There are many different ways to accomplish the entire length of the divide. Some have done the entire 672 miles nonstop, with either supply caches made ahead of time or friends meeting them at prearranged passes. Others have only been able to do short sections at a time, connecting them together in whatever order was most practical. In all cases, however, unlike usual backpack journeys, the ending point is usually never the same as the beginning. One must be prepared for unforeseen trouble along the way in the form of sickness, injury, weather, or just plain fatigue. It may not be possible simply to go back down the trail to your car, and it may well be necessary to leave the divide through unfamiliar territory or to make camp in almost any kind of terrain.

One of the first considerations of any extended trip is to know the personalities and capabilities of your partners. While some people may get along very well together on a weekend outing, journeys of a great distance and time may prove trying it not downright miserable. Some of the divide expeditions mentioned in this book successfully completed treks that went virtually nonstop for eight weeks, covering a distance of nearly 700 miles! When people must get along well with one another under the sometimes stressful conditions of high altitude, bad weather, time schedules, fatigue, injury, and numerous other unforeseen problems, extra effort must be put forth by everyone to prevent the breakdown of human relations. If every member of the party will simply do everything possible to insure that everyone else has a good time, helping each other when necessary, success will be achieved. One of the most important plans that must be agreed upon ahead of time is to have a designated leader for the expedition.

One book that I highly recommend studying is *The Wilderness Handbook* by Paul Petzoldt. As organizer of the National Outdoor Leadership School, Petzoldt covers all aspects of survival, expedition behavior, food, hiking and climbing techniques, clothing, and equipment needed for safe and enjoyable backcountry travel.

In my personal account, I often mention the use of CB walkie-talkies to keep in contact with our drivers and for use as a static detector. The CB made the trips more enjoyable for both hiker and driver as we kept track of each other's progress. It served particularly well of course on those occasions that weather dictated a change of plans and we could tell our drivers where to meet us. The static detection was a fascinating experiment and taught us much about the nature of ground to cloud electrical charges and how to seek an area of safety from possible lightning strikes. If you care to add the extra weight and bulk of a CB unit, I suggest something of at least three to five watts, equipped with the popular channel 19 and emergency channel 9 crystals. A small AM-FM radio with a rod antenna will also serve as a static detector when set to the AM band.

Be certain that your equipment is well tested and broken in properly. Boots in particular can create the greatest hardship if they do not fit properly or have not been broken in beforehand. Adequate first-aid supplies are a must and in case of a foot blister, Tom and Judy Melzer recommend the use of vaseline soaked cotton, moleskin, and tape.

Clothing must be adequate for ANY kind of weather. Colorado will surely dish out all seasons on the divide ridge. Rain, sleet, hail, snow, wind, freezing cold temperatures, burning bright sunshine, and lightning will all be encountered. In addition, don't forget sunscreen, insect repellent, sunglasses, and skin lotion to help with the prolonged effects of sunshine and wind.

Almost everyone loves to take photographs of their hikes and climbs, but even the standard 35mm single-lens reflex can become a bulky and heavy burden on a long pack trip. The modern zoom/macro lenses offer a single lens that will do almost everything from wide-angle to telephoto. I have found that I use my pocket 35mm more and more. Many very fine pocket-size, full-frame 35mm cameras are now available and, although they are limited in their capabilities, they offer top quality photography and are a real pleasure to carry and use.

Proper maps for the divide are a must. Knowing how to orientate the map and to use the magnetic pole declination angle with a compass can be very useful and is essential on those portions of the divide ridge that are not so obvious. Everyone I have talked with agrees that some errors will be found on all maps. Sometimes trails are shown that no longer exist and new trails exist where none are shown. Permanent streams are marked in places that will be dry and one must not count on map indications for water supplies.

Water is one of the most important concerns for the divide hiker. Gone are the good old days when one could drink from mountain streams without concern. Now, giardia and other diseases may contaminate even the safest looking mountain water. I carry the "First Need" filter which sells for about $40 and has a replaceable charcoal filter. Numerous similar filters are now on the market and offer the safest way to obtain clean drinking water from almost any source. If you filter water that has a lot of silt, mud, or algae in it, let some stand for a while to settle the larger particles so that your filter won't become clogged.

Another important concern is a good backpacking stove, not only for efficient cooking, but also to avoid the heavy impact of campfires. Stoves come in two basic types — gasoline and propane/butane canister. The latter is easier to light and not as messy to use or refuel, but can prove inefficient in cold weather. I prefer a gas stove, finding them efficient no matter how cold the weather is. I currently use a Coleman Peak 1, but my old Primus self-generating stove still works like new after twenty-five years of use. The Peak 1 seems to withstand considerably more wind than the Primus or Svea style stove, although it is a bit larger and heavier. The most reliable fuel for the gas stoves is Coleman Fuel, readily available almost anywhere. Various sizes of aluminum fuel bottles are available and I have found that besides filling the stove itself, an extra pint will usually suffice for about three days and a quart will last from six to seven. It is wise to carry plenty of fuel, particularly if you plan on melting snow for water.

Food is the last item to cover here and is probably the most debatable subject of all. Most people immediately think of freeze-dried, packaged foods when planning a backpack trip. This method of dehydrating and packaging a variety of foods does have its limitations. Personally, I like many of the freeze-dry dinners and egg breakfasts and have used most of the items that Mountain House makes. Other backpackers don't like them at all or at least tire of them quickly. For a short hike, where you may be out only a few days, these foods are fine. A full length divide hike of two months is an entirely different story. One not only gets tired of freeze-dry, but also begins to lack necessary food items that are not present in such dinners. Fats are practically nonexistent and some people have complained about getting chilled easily, losing weight, and being constantly hungry. Most packaged and canned foods list the number of servings they make. I have always wondered how people can survive on such small portions! Most people, especially those who have been hiking all day, need much more. When planning your food supplies, know your personal needs and tastes.

Supermarkets carry many items that can be used for backpacking, many of which are similar to the freeze-dry dinners but far less expensive. I have found that may boxed items can be divided into smaller portions and placed in baggies to make dinners just the right size. Individually packaged soups, instant breakfasts, instant teas and coffees, and chocolates are great pack items. Tom and Judy Melzer's favorite meal was Kraft macaroni and cheese mixed with freeze-dried peas. Taking the time to be innovative and make menus of variety can make a long backpack much more enjoyable.

Most of the hikers in this book had people meeting them at drivable access points along the way. Those meetings were always occasions for special feasts of foods that could not be carried in a pack. All hikers looked forward to milk shakes, watermelon, hamburgers, and other goodies supplied by their friends and relatives. For a day or two after such meets, hikers often carried perishable items such as fresh eggs, sausage, cheese, and fruit. Then there came several more days of packaged foods. On my own hikes, we often had a driver meet us and take us down to an established camp where we shared some fine dinners and breakfasts.

Lunch usually consists of snacking along the way instead of having one large "lump" of food that requires digestive energy while hiking. Popular items are dried fruits, nuts, candy, varieties of trail mixes, jerky, crackers, cheeses, and sausages that do not require refrigeration. Wyler's drink mix has always been a favorite beverage of mine and before giardia worries a double concentrated mixture made delightful snowcones when poured over a cupful of clean snow.

I keep a checklist of all items used on a backpack trip so that when I load up my pack, I do not forget necessary items. While everyone's checklist is bound to be different in some respects, my list below should be a good starter for your own. The weight of my pack with all of the following items and food enough for three days is close to fifty pounds.

Kelty outside frame pack
small day pack
hiking boots
lightweight tennis shoes
extra wool and light socks
sleeping bag
tent
Thermarest mattress
rain poncho
wool stocking cap
white cap (for sunny day)
light gloves
down mittens
light down jacket
nylon mountain parka
light nylon parka
appropriate extra clothing
Peak 1 stove
nylon/aluminum stake stove shield
stove starting jelly
aluminum fuel bottle/extra fuel
cook pot set and fry pan
knife, fork & spoon set
Swiss army knife
waterproof matches
propane lighter
magnesium "metal match"
water bottles

water pump filter
sierra cup
bottle of Vegaline
salt/pepper
can opener ("K" ration type)
fuel filter for stove
flashlight with extra lamp & batteries
biodegradable soap
scour pad
toilet paper
sunscreen
insect repellent
toothbrush and toothpaste
sunglasses
compass
first aid kit
pocket space blanket
thermometer
maps
notebook/pen
wire saw
pocket FM stereo radio/cassette
button type earphones for above
camera, film, pocket tripod
light nylon cord
candles
Cyalume chemical lightsticks
plastic trash sack
whistle on neck cord
fishing equipment (sometimes)
binoculars
extra food tubes and baggies

▲

Appendix E

Recommended Reading

Arps, Lousia Ward, and Elinor Eppich Kingery
High Country Names
Sage Books, 1966.

Bonney, Orrin and Lorraine
Guide to the Wyoming Mountains and Wilderness Areas
Sage Books, 1960.

Borneman, Walter R., and Lyndon J. Lampert
A Climbing Guide to Colorado's Fourteeners
Pruett Publishing Company, 1978.

Boyer, David S.
"Pride of Two Nations, Waterton-Glacier International Peace Park"
National Geographic Magazine, June 1987.

Eichler, George R.
Colorado Place Names
Johnson Publishing Company, 1977.

Garratt, Mike, and Bob Martin
Colorado's High Thirteeners, A Climbing and Hiking Guide
Cordillera Press, 1984.

Jacobs, Randy
Guide to the Colorado Trail
The Colorado Trail Foundation, 1988.

Koch, Don
The Colorado Pass Book
Pruett Publishing Company, 1980.

McIntyre, Loren
"The High Andes — South America's Islands in the Sky"
National Geographic Magazine, April 1987.

Ormes, Robert M.
Guide to the Colorado Mountains
The Colorado Mountain Club, 1983.

Robbins, Michael
High Country Trail Along the Continental Divide
The National Geographic Society, 1981.

Rosebrough, Robert F.
The San Juans Mountains, A Climbing and Hiking Guide
Cordillera Press, 1986.

Ryback, Eric and Tim
**The Ultimate Journey, Canada to Mexico Down the
    Continental Divide**
Chronicle Books, 1973.

Sprague, Marshall
The Great Gates, The Story of the Rocky Mountain Passes
Little, Brown and Company, 1964.

Wolf, James R.
Guide to the Continental Divide Trail
Volumes 3 and 4, Continental Divide Trail Society, 1982.

▲

Index

▲

Other Outdoor Books from Cordillera Press

ARIZONA'S MOUNTAINS
A Hiking and Climbing Guide
Bob and Dotty Martin

COLORADO'S HIGH THIRTEENERS
A Climbing and Hiking Guide
Bob Martin and Mike Garratt

COLORADO'S OTHER MOUNTAINS
Selected Peaks Under 14,000 Feet
Walter R. Borneman

MEXICO'S COPPER CANYON COUNTRY
A Hiking and Backpacking Guide
M. John Fayhee

THE SAN JUAN MOUNTAINS
A Climbing and Hiking Guide
Robert F. Rosebrough

TAKE 'EM ALONG
Sharing the Wilderness with your Children
Barbara J. Euser

▲